Th

TIDE TIME

By the same author

JUNE OF ROCHESTER
Edward Arnold & Co

TIDE TIME

A. S. BENNETT

LONDON
GEORGE ALLEN & UNWIN LTD
RUSKIN HOUSE MUSEUM STREET

386.3

———

TO JOHN WATERHOUSE
AND HIS CRONIES

———

PRINTED IN GREAT BRITAIN
in 11 *on* 12 *pt. Times Roman type*
BY BRADFORD & DICKENS
LONDON, W.C.I.

CONTENTS

ILLUSTRATIONS

ACKNOWLEDGMENTS

Certain chapters of this book have, in a slightly different form, already appeared in *Trident, Sail, Yachting World* and *Yachting Monthly*, under the initials " A B."

CHAPTER I

JUNE'S SWANSONG

June lay at anchor in the bight of the River Medway close under Cockham Woods. The sun was already rising over the Hoo Marshes and the morning mist was beginning to lift from the river.

From my hammock slung between the shrouds I gazed dreamily aloft to the fluttering bob 70-ft. up. It was pleasant day-dreaming there under the blankets. *June* was a comfortable old barge. Built at Murston in 1869, with some of her timbers reputedly worked in from old wooden battleships broken up after the Crimean war, she had spent all her workaday life in the cement trade sailing between Thames and Medway, until we bought her in 1933 and converted her to a yacht.

They must have looked after her well in the old days; we had done our best with her, too, during the seven years we had lived aboard. That 50-ft. sprit of Oregon pine, with that curious spiral grain glistening in the sun, we had found lying in the mud, covered in green slime. The pitch-pine mainmast had come from the old *Loo*—one of the last of the swim-headed barges. We had rigged those spars ourselves and dressed the sails on the grass each spring with fish oil and red ochre. More than once Dorothy and I had struggled aboard with a newly dressed mainsail to emerge from beneath the snaky coils like Red Indians.

We should have to find her a new mainsail soon. From my snug berth I could see where the canvas was chafed and worn in way of the main brails. The topsail, too, was getting on in years. . . .

My reverie was broken by a slow realization of a weight on my feet. I stirred and a cold damp nose nuzzled under the bed-clothes after my hand.

"So, it's you, is it, you rascal! Come on. Out you come."

There was a momentary upheaval, and a black-and-tan terrier scrambled over my chest to leap on to the cabin top.

1

He stretched himself luxuriously, first the front paws, then the back. A quick shake, and he was wide awake, with ears and tail erect.

"I suppose you want to go ashore?"

Chimp yelped and wagged his tail so violently that his feet skidded on the smooth, painted cabin top. Then, as I crawled out from the hammock he ran aft and stood with his paws on the quarter rail mesmerizing the boat.

I, too, stretched myself, and strolled forward to take down the riding light. Dorothy opened an eye when I went below to dress, then feigned sleep again.

"Shan't be long," I murmured. "Just taking Chimp ashore for a run. Tide'll be going soon."

Chimp jumped into the boat and stood in the bows like a figurehead. Before the boat had grounded he was in the water and streaking up the beach for the woods.

June was swinging to the ebb as we came off, and barges were already under way in Chatham Reach. Dorothy met us at the companion hatch.

"I thought you were in a hurry to get off?"

"So I am," for we were bound away down for Conyer Creek in the East Swale. "But not before breakfast, though!"

Chimp pricked up his ears, then scampered to the galley port and sniffed appreciatively.

"Will breakfast be long?" I asked.

Just then Chimp came dashing aft, pushed his way between us and jumped down the companion ladder.

"What's bitten him?" I began, but Dorothy only smiled.

"He's like the rest of you men when he sees food on the table."

*   *   *   *   *

After breakfast, while Dorothy squared off below, I began to shorten in. We lay to a shackle and a half, and with very little strength yet in the ebb it came in easily enough, for a barge's windlass is such a massive, well-geared affair that one man can normally break out the anchor unaided. I took my time, pausing to sluice water over the chain as it lay on deck and flaking down on the headledge grating.

When Dorothy came on deck she found me leaning against

2

the windlass bitts watching the *East Anglia* sailing past, a well-found barge fresh from the yard.

" Busy? " said Dorothy.

" Just waiting for courage."

A true bargeman never seems to hurry. What is more, he makes the barge do the work. He has to, for a deep-loaded barge is a heavy craft for two men to sail summer and winter.

Dorothy unlashed the hammock and dropped it below through the cabin hatch, while I cast off the topsail clewline and hauled out the sheet.

" Ouch! "

I ducked as rainwater poured from the folds of the topsail, much to Dorothy's amusement. It is surprising what does come out of the topsail after being furled for any length of time; we had birds nesting there more than once!

The sound of the patent blocks as a barge's topsail creeps slowly up the mast makes sweet music on a summer's morning. It can be heavy work though, with wind in the sail. The last few inches are the worst. Of course, the halyards could be led to the mast winch, but I have been chary of that since the day at Fambridge when I blithely hove away on the winch because the topsail seemed unduly heavy, only to find the canvas was nipped in the main brail block. The topsail went up, but only at the expense of a 3-ft. rent in the tack that gave me a couple of hours uncomfortably perched aloft on the crosstrees with palm and needle. Since then I prefer making fast the halyard and sweating the topsail close up with a foot braced against the mast.

This morning there was no hitch. The headstick climbed steadily up, and the heavy canvas flapped gently in the breeze. I bowsed down the tack, then got the last inch or so on the sheet.

" What about the mains'l? " Dorothy asked. " Are you set-ting that now? "

" We'll give her a few cloths. Take the block aft if you like."

I cast off uppers and lowers and eased away the main brail on the small crab winch, then went aft to help Dorothy hook the block on the traveller and mouse it.

" Well, that's about the lot. Shan't want the mizzen just yet.

3

You might let go the kicking strap, though, and try out the rudder."

The kicking strap is a small chain leading inboard from the rudder and set up against the wheel. This stops the barn door of a rudder from slamming about on its pintles, which it is apt to do in the quietest night anchorage and reverberate through the ship.

The boat was already made fast astern; I lowered the lee-boards a foot or so to keep them quiet, and eased off the vangs. Dorothy had the wheel; she was already sitting in her favourite position on the stern cabin top.

"What d'you want me to do?" she asked.

"Just keep her steady the way she lies until the anchor's aweigh, then hard a-port."

The foresail was already made up barge-fashion and hoisted halfway up the forestay. I cast off all but the last turn of the clewline and made fast the bowline to the starboard shroud.

Breaking out the anchor was a more strenuous business. Twice *June* took a sheer and snubbed at her chain. I had to wait for her, then away it came.

"Hard over," I yelled, and dashed to hoist the foresail. The great bag of a sail filled a-weather.

June paid off slowly. I made fast the foresail tack and hove the anchor right up, only to find the flukes fouling the stem. Veering a fathom or so will sometimes clear it; not so this time, for I had to go overside and jump about on the stock before the fluke came clear and the anchor lay comfortably a-cock-bill.

We were clear now of the anchorage and slipping past the lovely old three-masted topsail schooner *Rhoda Mary*. I let go the foresail bowline, and the traveller clanged its way lazily over the iron horse. There was no great strength in the wind, and to set the mainsail I lifted the pawl of the main brail winch to shake it out with a run.

Dorothy sailed *June* down past Gillingham and through Pinup Reach with the old forts on either hand. The breeze was south-west, and we held the same gybe. I left her to it; there was plenty for me to do on deck, and I can think of few more pleasant ways of passing a forenoon. *June* looked well in spite of her years, tarred hull set off with grey-blue decks

4

and buff-coloured cabin tops, dark green rails and transom, and varnished teak coamings with ports picked out in green. All the sails were newly dressed, and masts and spars bright-varnished. As usual, we had fitted her out ourselves in the spring, with a few days on the blocks at Strood to have the bottom scraped and re-nailed where necessary. We had given her another coat of tar just a week back on the beach at Upnor, making fast to the trees in a time-honoured spot. She was fairly tight both above and below water, but, like all old craft, needed constant care. Decks had to be kept well painted and washed down regularly night and morning. There was always some job on hand; under the chain grating alone, we had worked in seven new lengths of 2½-in. planking. Provided she is looked to regularly and kept well tarred, a barge's hull is unlikely to give much trouble, but decks and gear always need attention, and, while we enjoyed looking after *June,* it was hard work nevertheless.

There was a sparkle on the water and a nip in the air as we sailed down river that morning. The Medway may not be attractive in the same way as the Essex and Suffolk rivers, but the low-lying deserted saltings, intersected by innumerable, winding creeks, have a beauty all their own. I learned my sailing in these waters in a small spritsail-rigged skiff-dinghy of some antiquity; Yantlet, Hoo, Otterham, Stangate and the rest of the creeks conjure up many happy memories. They were once far more than muddy, meandering gutways, as remains of old barge wharfs, strayways and hards will testify. When barges were in their heyday, there was plenty of life in these parts; deserted they may be, but I find them attractive still, even to the rotting barge hulks propping up the sea walls, earth-filled mostly, and overgrown with grass and wild thyme.

Presently, as we drew clear of Sheerness Harbour—the Ness to bargemen—I set up the topmast backstay and hoisted our staysail, 50-ft. on the luff and a fine powerful sail in a light breeze. A couple of barges had come out from Queenborough ahead of us and were now gybing round the Grain Spit for the Jenkin's Swatch and London River. But our course lay seaward. With the red-and-white chequered West Cant buoy astern, we luffed up across the Flats.

"Keep about a mile offshore," I said. "There'll be water

5

enough for us, but I'll give her a bit more leeboard to give warning if we're standing in too far."

The sails needed trimming. I set the mizzen to balance the staysail, and hove in the mainsheet until *June* was sailing on the sheet, sprit well off to port, topsail and mainsail forming one great sweeping curve.

Presently Dorothy handed over the wheel and went below to prepare lunch, while I brought *June* along the coast past Minster Cliffs and Warden Point. *June* really sailed herself; there was little for me to do but sit back and soak in the sunshine.

There was the choice of two channels into the East Swale. We could stand on for the Columbine Spit buoy off Whitstable and beat up the main channel between the Columbine and Pollard Spit. Alternatively, we could luff up past Leysdown and try to cheat the tide through Ham Gat.

I put it to Dorothy when she came on deck again with sandwiches and lemonade.

" . . . . Of course, there might not be water for us in Ham Gat."

"Would it matter much?"

"Not particularly. We'd have to bring up off Harty for a bit, anyway. Of course, we could anchor down by the Columbine for that matter and wait for the flood."

Just then Chimp bestirred himself from his coil of rope. He pricked up his ears, then leaped out and stood with his front paws on the quarter rail sniffing at the shore.

We both smiled.

"That's settled it," I said with a smile. "It will have to be Ham Gat, then. If you could hold her up a bit I'll get the sprit and mainsheet in."

When the leeboard touched, we bore away, skirting the R.A.F. gunnery range buoy before laying up close-hauled again.

"Touching!"

I hove up the leeboard a couple of feet. Again we touched. The Ham Gat buoy was now less than three cables off the port bow.

"We'll be in the deep channel again once we're past the buoy," I muttered as I sweated on the leeboard tackles.

6

We just failed to make it. Sailing her full and by, we had the buoy almost abeam when we stuck and the boat came gently nuzzling up alongside. Chimp thought it was for him and jumped in.

"Well," said Dorothy, shrugging her shoulders, "if we really are going to be here for a while I may as well take Chimp ashore."

I gave the sails a rough stow, leaving the topsail sheet hauled out and the mizzen still set, then let go the anchor. The stock showed clear of the water. It was pointless taking the boat, so we carried Chimp and paddled ashore.

Shell Ness is a pleasant place in summer, but in winter it must be dreary and desolate. Years ago barges brought up here waiting to make a passage across to Belgium and Holland, or hanging on for a slant to take them down channel to the Isle of Wight and the West country.

We were alone to-day, and spent the afternoon lying in the hammocks on deck. By four o'clock the tide was making up and we had swung to the flood. We made sail and hove up the anchor. It was a turn to windward now through the East Swale, and the breeze piped up as it so often does with a weather-going tide.

"We'll let her come. . . ."

Dorothy tends the foresail this time. *June* comes up majestically into the wind. The foresail kicks, then topsail and mainsail slat and slam. The mainsheet block becomes possessed of the devil. Now is the time to get that last pull on the mainsheet; it has to be quick, though. The mizzen, sheeted hard to the rudder itself, helps to sweep our stern round. Already *June* is head to wind; the foresail has a last sullen crack and fills aback, held by the bowline. The sprit lurches over. Topsail fills. Time now to ease the wheel.

"Righto! "

The foresail sweeps over, flogs a couple of times and is quiet. The mainsail is asleep once more. *June* is away on the fresh tack and the weather board is already streaming out. . . .

We had to beat up to Faversham Creek to clear the Horse, then filled on the port tack and lay up past Harty with the white Ferry Inn nestling under the green hillside. Some people

7

aboard a motor-cruiser just above the hard waved as if they knew us, but we were too far off to see them clearly.

It was a long leg and a short from Harty, and I toyed with the idea of working up to the entrance of Conyer Creek through South Deep inside Fowley Island, but at the last moment we caught sight of a mudbank just awash and bore away outside the Island. We found the mud just the same, and it was no easy job heaving the leeboard clear.

We came about on the starboard tack, but within a minute or two found yet another bank, for the Swale is full of banks and channels just hereabouts. Once more we winded, but had barely filled before the leeboard tackle again went slack. It was soft mud, with a vengeance. *June* ploughed her way through and the leeboards dropped again.

But we had had enough. Early on the tide, there was too little water for us over the banks into Conyer, and I ran forward to let go topsail and foresail.

"Let her come up," I shouted to Dorothy. "We'll sort things out afterwards."

June rounded up and I let go the anchor. There seemed quite a reasonable depth and I tried the lead to find two fathoms. We should be all right for the night, anyway.

Presently we sailed ashore in the boat to Butterfly Wharf and walked up Conyer Creek to the village. There we arranged for a local barge skipper to come off and help us up on the morning tide. We met friends, too, in other converted barges at the quay, *Mermaid, Waveney* and *Glasgow,* and it was almost dark when we got back on board.

That night I turned out once. It was low water and dark banks of mud showed on either side of us. But *June* lay quietly and the riding light burned brightly. It was a beautiful starlit night with dawn not so very far away. For a few minutes I stood in the hatchway listening to the marsh birds on Fowley. It was quite cold, though. I shivered and crept below.

Next morning we were under way in good time and stood across for the eastern end of Fowley Island. Our huffler was waiting in his boat, and together we worked *June* up the narrow, winding gut to berth at Conyer Quay.

It was Sunday morning—the last Sunday in August, 1939.

8

1 *June* sailing on a broad reach, with the 50-ft. Oregon pine sprit and the yard tackle band glistening in the sunshine.

2a *June*. The sprit or "spreet" is controlled by vangs. The mainsail brails up like a theatre curtain, the main brail leading to a small crab winch on deck, while uppers and lowers give a snug stow. Leeboards take the place of a keel for sailing to windward.

b We berthed *June* astern of *Mermaid* in the little dock at the head of Conyer Creek. That was in 1939. *Mermaid* is still there.

3   *Venture* is a 65-ft. motor fishing Drifter hailing from Peterhead.
She is back at the fishing now.   This photo was taken by the
Sub-Lieutenant aboard *Cranefly*.

4a Chief and the Skipper.

b Tommy Green and the Mate.

5 *H.M.M.L.* 1031, the first of the 72-ft. Diesel-engined M.L.s, on the slip at Lymington Shipyard.

6a H. M. M.L. 146 off Ramsgate just before paying off in August, 1945. Only Navigational Leaders attached to the Assault Forces carried the Radar tower amidships.

b Looking aft aboard M.L. 146, with Coxswain on the right. This was the Twin Oerlikon mounted above the Wardroom.

7 The Sea Wall, Whitstable, in winter, with *The Nore* on the left
and the Harbour beyond.

8*a* The view from our window. The barge on the Flats is *Major*, of Harwich, a fine big Channel barge, since rebuilt at Anderson's Yard.

b Elizabeth and Spanker look out on the Sea Wall. Spanker is the successor to Chimp, our little black and tan terrier who just outlived *June*.

CHAPTER II

POWDER BARGE

WAR was declared the following Sunday. It was part of our office Civil Defence scheme that half of us should remain at home. Like many others in the Royal Naval Volunteer Supplementary Reserve, I was expecting to be called up at any moment, but after a few days, with life in the brickfields and farms and village continuing in much the same old way and still no telegram from the Admiralty, I began to get restive.

I telephoned the office for instructions. It seemed that shipping was in very much of a flux. "There's no point in your coming up to London," said my chief. "Can you make yourself useful where you are?"

My thoughts naturally turned to barges; I had heard of a shortage of mates, and got into touch with the London & Rochester Trading Company, at Strood. It seemed that their *Vera* was lying at Upnor without a mate. . . .

So it was on Sunday morning just a fortnight after we had sailed away in *June* I was back in Upnor again, with a bag slung over my shoulder and hammock under my arm, explaining my way past the police on the gate of the powder jetty.

"*Vera*, chum? Why, she's out there on the buoy. You'll get a lift out to her from the jetty, I shouldn't wonder."

The mate of another barge put me off. *Vera* was outside barge of a tier of three, with tarred sides and severe black rail relieved only by a single gold band; 130-tonner or thereabouts and part-loaded. I threw my gear and scrambled aboard. Her decks were grey and freshly dressed; the rails inside were painted sea-green; lines were neatly flaked on the hatch tops. From first impressions she seemed a well-found barge.

I made my way aft and peered down the open cabin hatch.

The skipper was seated at the table peeling potatoes; a tall, spare man of about thirty-five, saturnine and rather morose in appearance.

9

"Come on down," he called, and while I introduced myself, he nodded and reached across the table for more potatoes.

The cabin followed the usual lines, with lockers and drawers set right aft in the Yarmouth Roads against the transom; built-in cupboard bunks on either side; horse-shoe locker seats around the hanging table; a coal range set against the forward bulkhead with mantelshelf and mirror above; while a glass-panelled door shut off the small hanging space and companion ladder on the port side.

The skipper was a man of few words. He pointed his knife towards the starboard bunk. "That's yours."

It struck me as odd, for the skipper traditionally sleeps in the starboard bunk. However, it was all the same to me, so I pushed back the sliding door and threw my bag in. It was quite clean inside except for a few spent matches.

I turned round to find the skipper watching me closely. "I reckon you'll want a mattress," he said quietly, then bent to his potato peeling again.

"That's all right," I replied. "I've got my hammock and I'll sling in the fo'c'sle for the time being. I see we're loaded."

The skipper nodded.

"When are we sailing?"

"Sailing?" he grunted. "Where to?"

"Why," I said, somewhat crestfallen. "Haven't we a job?"

"I reckon so. We're on charter at three quid a day to swing round the buoy. That's our orders from what I can see of it!"

We had cold meat and pickles with the potatoes for dinner, washed down with tea. Then the skipper sat back on the lockers with his feet hunched up, clasping his knees and watching from half-closed eyes while I cleared the table and washed up. When I looked up again he was asleep.

The *M.N.* lay alongside us on the buoy. Her mate was standing in the hatchway when I went on deck to empty the bowl of water.

"Going ashore?" he asked hopefully.

I shook my head. "I only came aboard this morning."

"I saw you come off. Stayin' on?"

I looked up quickly, bowl in hand. "And why not?"

"Oh, nothing," he said, drawing a finger down the side of

10

his nose. "Only the last bloke didn't go much on it. One night and he's off ashore."

"What was the trouble? Was it too slow for him? "

"Garn! " The mate looked round cautiously and lowered his voice to a dramatic whisper. "Bugs! "

I waited until the skipper had gone ashore before pursuing the subject further. Then the mate of the *M.N.* warmed to his subject.

"That's right what I'm tellin' you. Smart little kid an' all, but he couldn't stick 'em. Eaten up, he was! "

We went below and inspected the bunk. It was lined out with grey-painted matchboarding and there was nothing to be seen. The mate of the *M.N.* thrust his head inside and lit a succession of matches.

"Looks all right," he admitted grudgingly. "So it should the way Charlie was scrubbin' out fer a coupla days. Burnt sulphur candles an' fair stunk the place out."

"Maybe he got rid of them," I suggested hopefully.

But the mate only snorted and shook his head. "Not b—— likely, he didn't! Why, I reckon you'd have to strip down all that there lining to do the job properly, and even then you wouldn't be shot on 'em."

I took the boat ashore soon after ten o'clock to bring the skipper off. He had missed the bus and walked from Frindsbury with a bag of provisions on his shoulder. Over a cup of tea I tackled him about the bunk.

"Well, I've hopped out night-times and never seen a thing," he declared, sitting hunched up on the locker seat and staring morosely into the mug. Then grudgingly, as if reading his fortune in the tea leaves: "I know the cause of it all. It was that ol' —— what had the barge while I was ashore sick. This place was like a pigsty time I come off. He wasn't long packing his bag, I can tell you! "

He lapsed into silence, then sighed and looked up.

"I reckon you'll soon be off yourself? "

"Good heavens, no! " I hurriedly assured him. "I prefer a hammock, anyway."

Life aboard *Vera* was pleasant enough though uncommonly quiet. The skipper never completely thawed, but he was obviously relieved I was staying on, for a barge that cannot keep

11

her mate is looked on askance. He did most of the cooking, while I cleared away, scrubbed out the cabin and generally squared up. Otherwise there was little to do beyond trying the pumps and washing down the decks.

There was the usual traffic on the river, with work still for barges and coasters. Possibly Chatham Dockyard on the far side of the river was rather bare of craft, but there was little to proclaim a state of war. At night conditions were more realistic with blackout and searchlights; sleeping aboard a floating powder magazine was strange at first, but the tide slapping against our buoy and gurgling between bluff bows made homely sounds and soporific.

Tuesday morning, the skipper came off aboard looking quite cheerful, with orders to be alongside an ammunition ship first thing in the morning.

" Where's she laying? " I asked.

" Long Reach."

I had visions of a sail round to the Thames, but it was Long Reach in the Medway just below the forts.

" That's all right," said the skipper. " Make a change, anyway. Reckon we'll drop down on the ebb and lay off till morning."

After dinner I cast off our moorings. There was a light breeze from the south-west and we lay head to wind and tide. *Vera* was rigged in the same fashion as *June,* but the gear was heavier. I managed to set the topsail myself, though the skipper weighed in with a final heave on the halyard.

" Just a cloth or two o' the main," he said as he overhauled the mainsheet and ran the block aft. . . . " That'll do her. Now give her the fores'l."

I made fast the bowline to the starboard shroud and hoisted away.

" Leggo forrard when you like! "

Our bows swung out. The foresail filled aback. Soon we were slipping down Cockham Reach with sprit squared off. It was curious how empty the river seemed to be. The Reserve Fleet was at sea, but off the Bullnose was moored an old Thames lighter armed with Lewis guns to deal with low-flying attacks on the entrance to the Dockyard.

12

We held our gybe all the way down. Our steamer lay at the bottom of Long Reach, with barges clustered about her.

"We'll bring up to wind'rd of her," said the skipper, "and jest inside so's to be out o' the fairway. All right, get yer fores'l off."

I let go the foresail halyard and made the sail up roughly by passing a few turns of the clewline before hoisting clear of the windlass. Then we gybed over and stood in towards the Hoo Flats.

"Leggo tops'l. . . ."

The headstick came tumbling down. We rounded up.

"When you like."

The chain grated against our bows and we swung to our anchor. At slack water, while we were below at tea, there came a sudden crunching and grinding of fenders. I poked my head out of the hatch and found a launch alongside crowded with stevedores and the foreman standing in the bows.

"We want you alongside port side forrard," he shouted. "Going to start you first thing, so you can berth when you like."

I raised my hand in acknowledgment. The telegraph tinkled and the launch sheered off up river.

I passed on the orders to the skipper, who just nodded and spread himself another slice of bread and jam. Later he went on deck and sat on the cabin top. By the time I had cleared away there was quite a touch of autumn in the air.

"Finished?"

"Yes," I replied. "That's the lot."

The skipper stood up and stretched lazily. "May as well get moving then."

I hove up the anchor while the skipper set the topsail. He certainly could handle a barge, for he put her alongside the buff-funnelled steamer so quietly that we had to hail for some-body to take our lines.

She was just in from Crombie, a 700-tonner specially built for armament and ammunition work, with a single hatch. I spent the evening aboard, and was introduced for the first time to naval Kai, thick sweet chocolate later to beguile many a dreary middle watch. The second mate had been chief officer of a deep-sea tanker. It was the chance of regular home life

apparently that attracted him, although carrying high explosives on the coast in wartime seemed a grim prospect to me.

Until quite recent years all officers in the Naval Auxiliary vessels had to pass through the sailing barges in much the same way that Trinity House pilots had to serve their time in square rig. From the barges they went to the tugs, but the link is broken now, for the smart Government powder barges disappeared a few years before the war.

Before breakfast next morning the skipper and I uncovered by folding back the hatch cloths and stacking the covers. Soon we were taking aboard more five-inch shells and boxes of ammunition. They had us finished by midday, when, somewhat deeper and more sluggish, we started to turn up the Medway for Upnor.

Sailing a loaded barge was something novel to me, for *June* drew less than three feet without leeboards and was a light barge to all intents and purposes. It was amazing the way *Vera* soaked up to windward through Short Reach on the weather-going tide. Slower through the water, she made one board of it where *June* would have needed three. The worm steering, too, had quite a different feel to our old chain gear. There was no slack, of course, but I missed the kick of the wheel.

Coming into Upnor Reach, the skipper took the wheel.

"We'll run back over the flood," he said, and stood on past the four-masted training ship *Arethusa* before coming about. The breeze had been dropping all the way up. Now it grew fluky. For a while we just held our own, but at last the breeze died completely, and there was nothing for it but to let go the anchor well over by the Dockyard wall. We whistled hopefully, but the breeze had gone. The skipper looked more morose than ever and scowled aloft at the lifeless bob, muttering imprecations.

"May as well get sail off her for all the use it is."

We thought we might get a pluck across the river, but not a single tug came near us, and in the end I went away in the boat with every bit of line we had on board. It took us nearly two hours to warp ourselves to the buoy. We were tired and hungry, for we had gone without dinner. Hands on hips, the skipper grimaced for a few moments at the mass of line litter-

14

ing the foredeck, then left me to clear up while he set about stewing a rabbit and some green pears he had come by ashore.

Faced with yet another indefinite spell on the buoy, I began to get restive again. There was little to do and all day to do it in, which was not my idea of an active wartime job. There was no future in powder barges, and before long they were dispersed from Upnor and anchored singly down in Long Reach, Stangate and Half Acre Creek, where they were serviced by the tugs *Kestrel* and *Kathleen*. Occasionally one or other towed away to Upnor or to an H.M. ship, but for the most part they swung at their moorings with topmasts housed and their bottoms growing more and more foul as the weeks and months passed by.

There was talk at one time of each barge having an annual refit; they were going to be unrigged and the gear stowed below, so rumour had it. As it transpired, a barge was lucky to see the yard once in two years. Some never went on at all, and it was nothing unusual to grow two feet of weed and barnacles on the bottom. Little wonder the powder barges picked up the worm! The gear gradually rotted; the sails blew out. One barge lay in Stangate for three years until at last she was towed to Upnor and some of her boxes opened up for inspection. Then hatches were battened down again and she was towed to Half Acre Creek for yet another two years' sojourn.

It was a boring existence for the crews. Some worked week on and week off; others a fortnight. Winter time was particularly grim, for only sperm oil was allowed aboard and lamp glasses got broken and were practically impossible to replace. Naked lights, of course, were completely prohibited.

There is a story told of the superintendent who came to visit old Bill Court aboard *Foxhound*. A couple of lighted candles stood on the table. Nothing was said. They sat and chatted, then when it was time to go the superintendent very deliberately snuffed out the candles between finger and thumb and put them in his pocket.

It can be cold in winter time in the Lower Medway when the easterlies whistle across the flats and saltings. Like all sailors, bargemen love a good fug in the cabin and coal was always a problem in the powder barges. Aboard the *King*

they made use of the double bulkheads between cabin and hold for bunkers. Unfortunately the coal caught fire one day while the mate was away visiting in the boat, and it was only by luck that a couple of lightermen happened to be around to put it out. After that, the use of double bulkheads for coal was forbidden, and all woodwork had to be stripped from around the stove.

The superintendent must have had his hands full at times, for bargemen are notoriously independent by the very nature of their job. The senior skippers were expected to keep a weather eye open for offenders against the regulations, particularly in respect of leaving barges unattended. Policemen, the younger men called them.

Bill Boxall, mate of the *William Cleverley*, found himself alone on one occasion in spite of repeated requests through the tugs for another man to be sent down. At last he sent an ultimatum; relief or no relief, he was off ashore for the week-end. Back came word that he was on no account to leave the barge.

But Bill Boxall—self-styled Battling Bargeman from Bredhurst—had other ideas. He packed his bag and went away in the boat, knowing full well that the skipper of the nearby *New Acorn* was watching him from his cabin hatch.

Sure enough, a short while later the telephone rang in the superintendent's office.

"Just letting you know the mate of the *William Cleverley's* gorn ashore."

"He mustn't do anything of the sort," stormed the superintendent. "Tell him he's got to hang on till I get one of the mates from up here sent down."

"It's no good, gov'nor. He's ashore already."

There was silence for a few moments, then the superintendent wanted to know who it was telephoning.

Back came the unexpected reply: "It's the mate of the *William Cleverley* here. Thought I'd better let you know before some other b—— gets on the phone!"

Then there was the mate who could not stand the solitude. He packed his bag one day and went up on deck all dressed for shore. For a while he paced up and down waiting for the tug, then he began to get impatient.

16

" Come on, hurry up! " he shouted. " I've got to get ashore.
. . . That's right. Don't bother to come right alongside. Just
touch in and I'll jump for it. . . . Easy now! Here, hang on
while I get a fender."

He dropped his bag and dashed forward. " Can't have our
old barge knocked about," he declared cheerfully as he dropped
in a fender.

" Right you are, Skipper. All aboard! " He grabbed his
bag and tossed it across, then with a cheery wave of his hand
he stepped lightly from the barge's rail.

Unfortunately that mate suffered from hallucinations. There
was no tug anywhere in the offing. Mad Joe was in the water
again!

I never reached such straits. After a few more days languish-
ing on the buoy at Upnor, I became doubled up with stomach
pains and was taken off to St. Bartholomew's Hospital, Rochester, at that time being held in readiness for Service casualties.
As an emergency case I was duly admitted with appendicitis.
The skipper came along later with my week's wages of £2 10s.
He looked at me gravely as I lay there in bed, then nodded
his head and tiptoed away.

Three days later I walked out. My appendicitis turned out
to be colic—or so it was thought. Warmed-up rabbit and green
pears may have had something to do with it!

Rather than go back to the powder work, I got myself a
berth as mate aboard a fine-looking barge newly fitted out at
Sittingbourne. The cabin was a picture, and the dear old white-
haired skipper was very proud of it.

But I never joined her, for my office decided to recall me
until such time as My Lords Commissioners of the Admiralty
required my services.

CHAPTER III

VENTURE

I JOINED H.M.S. *King Alfred*, the R.N.V.R. Officers' Training Establishment at Hove, early in November, 1939.

Lateres sine Sramento was later adopted as the semi-official motto of *K.A.*, and incurred the displeasure of their Lordships —so it was rumoured. "Bricks without straw" was certainly appropriate in those early days, but the instructors were excellent and their improvisation remarkable. We were a keen lot, too. Bewitched and bewildered, I jumped to it with the rest of my class in the battery. I doubled round obsolete guns smartly and uncomprehendingly, but while others pressed forward to strip down breech block mechanism, I hung about on the fringes; when volunteers were called to put the pieces together again I made myself small and kept very quiet.

At signals I confessed to a nodding acquaintance with the Morse code and was put in the advanced section, but as soon as the light began to blink on the wall I surreptitiously joined the beginners.

An old white-haired chief petty officer took us for anchor work, going through the drill with the aid of a model battleship's foredeck. Another took us for boat drill. We tackled navigation, too. I, who had boxed *June* around with obsolete charts and a compass set against the after coaming just forward of the iron wheel, now glimpsed for the first time something of the mysteries of deviation and variation. I had to work in degrees now instead of points. No longer was it permissible to lay off a course with the edge of a book; nor could I hold her up a couple of points for leeway and a bit for tide; there were such things as tide-triangles to trap the unwary. I never imagined such desperate problems in coastal navigation.

Depth charges appealed to me. The ingenious simplicity of the pistol mechanism was enhanced by the lucidity of our instructor, and I retained a warm regard for depth charges until a year or so later one achieved the impossible by going

off almost as soon as it hit the water, giving me a shaking and accounting for thirty-six of my M.L.'s keel bolts.

Field training was something of a high spot; C.P.O. Vass enlivened our instruction with wit and comment that came to endear him to thousands. As newly commissioned sub-lieutenants, we were inclined to address him as " Sir."

" Now let's get this straight," he would say. " It's taken me twenty years to get where I am. Chief, that's me. *And* I'm proud of it! "

I formed the opinion in those early days, which subsequent years only served to strengthen, that the petty officers and chief petty officers are the backbone of the Royal Navy.

I became convinced, too, of my complete ignorance of all things pertaining to the Service. Yet, strangely enough, at the end of a fortnight, when I received my first appointment to H.M. motor drifter *Venture,* in command, I felt no serious qualms.

Bricks without straw! H.M.S. *King Alfred* was certainly unique in its way.

There were three of us appointed to drifters, and the naval officer in charge greeted us benignly. Apparently there was reason to believe the Germans were contemplating a surface raid on Dundee, with its considerable shipbuilding yards and docks, and we were to constitute the first line of defence.

It sounded most impressive, and N.O.I.C. must have been amused at our serious faces, for he stood up and smiled. " Well, I know you'll want to get aboard, so I'll run you down to the docks in the car. We've done the best we can for you by way of accommodation. I hope you'll like them." Then, as an afterthought: " I was in trawlers myself last war."

Venture, Viola and *Suilven* lay in the dock hemmed in by dozens of craft in various stages of repair and conversion; typical, modern, East Coast of Scotland motor drifters; sturdily built 65-ft. double-enders, with a bold sheer and considerable freeboard. *Venture* was reputed to be a sister-ship of the *Girl Pat* that went missing from the herring fishing before the war to reappear weeks later in South American waters.

The crew were already aboard and throwing bashful, side-long glances to know what manner of naval officer the "Admirality" had sent them. Six were T-124 fishermen from

the Peterhead district, sailing under ordinary Merchant Service Articles, but subject to naval discipline. There were skipper and mate, engineer, cook and two seamen. The skipper ranked as chief petty officer; mate as petty officer, and so on, each being issued with a uniform appropriate to his rate, and which, needless to say, they were somewhat diffident of wearing. Jerseys and slouch caps were the rig of the day when I stepped aboard in all the glory of my new gold braid, to be smartly saluted by a two-badge leading seaman hailing from the Clyde Division R.N.V.R., also decked out in his No. 3's. His job, it appeared, was to look after our four depth charges and single Lewis gun which constituted our main armament. We also carried a revolver and two rather ancient Lee-Enfield rifles.

I had hardly time to get my gear below to the tiny cabin built in the fish hold when we were required to shift berth to take aboard dan buoys. The engineer—invariably dubbed Chief—dived below and started up the 66-h.p. National diesel engine. All controls were in the wheelhouse, and he explained how they worked in a broad Scottish accent. The reverse gear lever was to starboard of the wheel and throttle to port.

"An' mind ye ease her doon afore ye let her oot o' gear!"

I gathered, too, that if the oil pressure gauge dropped below ten I had to call him out, otherwise dreadful things were likely to happen to his beloved engine. He then stuffed his hands in his pockets, and the skipper and I eyed each other diffidently. It was the skipper's job to shift in dock—or was it? He cheerfully admitted to a lack of experience in ship handling. Nor had I any pretensions, for the only time I had the wheel of a powered craft was aboard a motor cruiser towing a sprit for *June* from Kingsferry Bridge in the River Swale up to Rochester, when I nearly dropped off to sleep!

The Chief saw how matters lay. "Ach! I ken her fine," he murmured with a disarming grin.

He jammed in the gears, worked ahead and astern, shouted a few completely unintelligible commands to the deckhands, and gradually the solid phalanx of craft opened up and we backed out into the dock. Then we turned short round and nosed up to the quay. I watched him carefully to see how it was done, for all this was new to me.

20

He turned to me with a smile and whispered confidentially, "She's a bonny wee ship. We'll dae fine."

Jock Hay was my mainstay throughout that first winter of the war. Not only did he know his job thoroughly as engineer, but his was a varied experience. Youngest boy in trawlers in the 1914/18 war, he later went into salvage work, worked up to quartermaster in deep-sea cargo liners, became lighthouse keeper, then cook, mate, deckhand, skipper, fireman and engineer in trawlers. Finally he took to diesel engines, and had been in *Venture* for several years. Always in the offing when advice was most needed, he took me quietly and unobtrusively under his wing.

We patrolled the Tay Approaches by day and the lower reaches of the river by night, two drifters relieving each other every eight hours. Our time off as stand-by ship was usually spent sleeping at anchor off Buddon High Light, where a signal station had been established. At the end of four days we put back to Dundee for one clear day and two nights in port.

We took our patrols seriously, for the Bar at the mouth of the Tay has as bad a reputation as any in the British Isles. It can blow a gale of wind from the south-west with little or nothing to show for it, but an easterly breeze soon knocks up a wicked sea with white-capped combers. At Springs, with a six-knot ebb and a north-easterly gale, the seas break heavily on the Bar with a roar that can be heard for miles.

We were lucky to have a spell of decent weather at the start. Then, running out on the ebb one morning just before Christmas, we found the breeze was in the east. I had the wheel and the Chief came up to stand quietly behind me.

"Watch y'sel'," he whispered.

We must have been doing about fourteen knots over the ground. Before I realized it we were driving into one of the steepest seas I had ever met. There was barely time to yell a warning to the hands on deck before we were submerged under a towering, white-crested wall of water. The worst of it seemed to go clean over the wheelhouse and flooded out the cabin aft.

"Keep her goin'," murmured the Chief without batting an eyelid. "But ease her richt doon fer the next yin."

21

I nursed her out over the Bar. *Venture* dipped her bows in once or twice, but I had the feel of her now. When I looked round, the Chief had gone; he was down below soothing the cook and helping to clear up the mess.

Venture was light and lively, but a magnificent seaboat. The foremast had been taken out of her, but we regularly set the mizzen, sheeted well home, and it served to steady her in a seaway. Even so, our leading seaman, who had spent much time on Mediterranean cruises with the Fleet, was laid up with seasickness for the first two weeks out.

I had a present of thirty shillings from my London office with which to celebrate the New Year on board. We came in from sea at four o'clock on New Year's Eve, and instead of bringing up off Buddon, the cook prevailed on me to put into Tayport, about five miles up river, to enable him to lay in provisions for the feast.

We berthed soon after five o'clock, and the cook stepped ashore, to return well laden with a chicken, sausages, haggis and a vast collection of nuts and other dainties. Then most of the others went ashore ostensibly to the pictures and with strict instructions to be back by ten o'clock, as we were due to relieve *Viola* at midnight.

Now, I had heard of Hogmanay, of course, but I never really appreciated its significance to the Scots. The skipper and mate were early aboard, but the others found friends ashore, so they said. The Chief dropped down the ladder at ten o'clock rather the worse for wear and turned in, but the clocks were striking midnight as the leading seaman and the two deck-hands came singing their way along the railway line. It was dead low water and the bottom rungs of the oily ladder were missing. They swung down part of the way and fell the rest.

"Start up, Chief! " I bawled.

There was a convulsive flutter under the patchwork quilt, and a towsled head emerged from the bunk.

" Fit it is? "

"Come on, Chief. Start up."

He fell out of his bunk like a sack of potatoes and charged past into the engine room. There came hammerings and imprecations; to my amazement and relief, the engine burst into life.

22

We kept Hogmanay next day off Buddon, a much chastened but well satisfied ship's company, for the cook had done us well.

We used Tayport occasionally for our stand-by spell if the weather was bad. On one occasion it was blowing hard easterly and raining as we came in soon after midnight. It was low water, too. There were no lights showing, but we found our way up the channel through the flats and started to round up inside the harbour by going hard aport and full astern. To my horror, we hit the quay very nearly head on.

The Chief came into the wheelhouse and felt around the foot of the gear lever. " She was never in at a'," he said, as he pulled away bits of coir matting. " Ach, dinna fash. She can tak it! "

But I was worried. " I've a good mind to go out and bring her in again."

" Guid idea," he grinned, and rubbed his hands.

The skipper and one or two of the others thought it anything but a good idea, and said so. I told them to turn in, and out we went. All hands stayed on deck, I noticed. This time we crept in and berthed without further incident.

Later it transpired that the clutch lining had gone, and finally we had to go into dock. The engineers took the opportunity to give us a top overhaul, and in due course *Venture* was secured alongside for dock trials. All went well. It was then that N.O.I.C. had a signal from the Admiralty that drifters unable to attain a speed of eight knots were to be considered unsuitable for naval service. *Viola* and *Suilven* were slightly faster than *Venture*.

" They're all right," said N.O.I.C. " It's you I'm worried about. You'll have to run trials over the measured mile, and I want you to push her along all you can."

I had grown fond of *Venture* and had no wish to lose my first command. The Chief merely grinned when I told him.

" Ach, she'll dae it. We'll manage."

And so he did, but on the final run through the tide there came a strong smell of burning wood, and the Chief bustled up to pass the end of the deck hose down through the engine-room skylight.

" Are you all right? " I asked anxiously.

He nodded and disappeared again. At the end of the run I eased back the throttle and looked below.

"The bulkhead caught fire," said the Chief. "Dinna fash. She's a'richt."

Then we gave the reverse gear a thorough testing. We backed and filled and turned short round. At last we were satisfied and put back to land the engineers and their gear.

I stopped as we came through the entrance, and let her run her way off across the dock. Then hard over and full astern. The engine raced. *Venture* sailed gaily on with a following breeze. There was no time to get the anchor overside; I could only yell for fenders and hold on tight before we hit the quay practically head on. *Venture* shuddered and nearly whipped her mast out.

While the engineers were at work I had the top of the wheel-house recanvased. The workmen found a bar of metal screwed down on the starboard side and well covered with several layers of paint. I must have vaguely connected it with the overhead compass, for I bade them replace it in exactly the same position.

When eventually we got away again on patrol, I was amazed to find the compass out by several points on some courses, and made a signal for it to be adjusted. N.O.I.C. came down himself to witness such a phenomenon. He demanded a leg-up and clambered on top of the wheelhouse. Then he called for a screwdriver.

"Are you sure this corrector magnet hasn't been moved?"

So that was what it was! I assured him it was replaced in exactly the same position; in fact they had picked up the old screw holes.

N.O.I.C. had taken off the bar and was making passes over the compass. Then he started to screw it down again.

"You're quite right," he said at last with a disarming smile. "It's where it should be, only they've put it back the wrong way round."

We saw the first mine go up off Dundee early in 1940. A motor drifter was returning home from the herring fishing in the Firth of Forth, and had just passed across the line of the Tay Approach buoys, when a great column of water shot

24

up astern. I thought at first she had dropped a depth charge with a shallow setting.

"Fit it is?" shouted the skipper, his eyes popping out of his head. "I've never seen the like afore."

"Yon's a mine," the Chief replied, and we watched with amazement while the eruption slowly subsided. "Like as not the wee drifter set it aff."

We marked the spot with a dan buoy and gave chase to the drifter to get his story.

"He's skeert and awa' hame," said the Chief, and went below to tinker with his engine. Black exhaust came forth in clouds and *Venture* throbbed and rumbled to a deeper note, but the other had too long a lead and was making for Arbroath.

"Fancy letting a little chap like that get away from us," I said to the Chief teasingly, as I eased down and headed for Buddon to report.

But the Chief merely shook his head and grinned. "Aye, but dinna forget yon's hae the de'il under his tail!"

It was surprising how quickly the ship settled down to the patrol routine. A good lookout was the essence of our job, and there were invariably three of us on deck. We made a crow's nest in the bows of large motor tyres that served as fenders; in a seaway it could be quite exhilarating perched there, for, being light and with plenty of freeboard, *Venture* rode each sea, rising high one moment, then down, down, down, until it seemed she could never pick up in time. We had little or no flare forward, yet we seldom had green water aboard.

As fishermen, the crew were used to long hours on deck, and night watches never troubled them. Many a time I stood behind Tommy Green, our burly Peterhead deck hand, as he sat motionless, a muffled figure wedged in the tyres, and wondered if he had drifted off to sleep. After five or ten minutes, just as I imagined the worst, maybe there would come a flurry on the water ahead and Tommy would ejaculate "Jukes!"

There were in fact great flocks of eider duck in the estuary, and they made an extraordinary noise scuttling across the water.

During the day there was plenty of interest, but at night inside the Bar, where we maintained a patrol whatever the weather, it became something of a nightmare at times. Fog,

snow and rain often obscured the dimly-lit buoys, and the strong tide with a pronounced set on the ebb over the sands towards St. Andrew's Bay was a constant anxiety.

We did go aground once on hard sand during the middle watch and dried out. We laid out our anchor and watched the rising wind with some apprehension. The sand felt like rock and we bumped unpleasantly for what seemed an age before we got off, luckily without damage.

We hit a buoy, too, one dark night, but for the most part we contrived to keep out of serious trouble.

I tackled the Paymaster-Commander during the cold spell on the question of rum. There was some doubt apparently whether T-124 ratings were entitled to draw.

" But it's essential," I persisted. " It's no joke, I assure you, keeping a watch on deck in a small ship this sort of weather."

" All right," he declared at last. " I'll probably be hung for it. Better call it medicinal! "

Thereafter the issue of a tot to those who wanted it after a cold or wet patrol became a highly irregular but none the less welcome feature.

The cold spell lasted for several months. A hard frost by night persisted, but the midday sun began to gather strength so that one day towards the end of February, out on patrol to the southward of the Bell Rock, we fetched up the paint pots and began to touch up the ship's boat on the hatch top.

It was quite hot, and I peeled off layers of jerseys and mufflers, until within a little I was stripped to the waist much to the amusement of Tommy Green, whose sole concession to the sparkling sunshine was to doff his cap.

It was the mate's watch, and he leaned out of the wheelhouse window chatting with the Chief, who stood lounging against the door jamb in his usual hunched-up position.

Presently I straightened up, brush in hand, and stretched luxuriously. There was a trawler on the port bow, and I turned to point her out to the mate.

"Aye," he said. " Yon's *Ben Attow*, sir. I've made a note in the log. Heavin' in her gear an' a'."

Sure enough, there was a white plume at her steam pipe and gulls wheeling around.

" Noo's the time to git a fry," murmured the Chief.

26

The old *Ben Attow* was a chummy ship, working out of Dundee, and she always had a bucket of fish for us whenever we cared to go alongside, so we altered course and bore down on her as she lay stopped, with her green, rust-streaked sides dipping lazily in the long swell. The Chief held up a bucket and her skipper beckoned to us cheerfully.

"Shall I touch in, sir?" asked the mate.

"Yes, please," I replied, then suddenly caught sight of another trawler inshore and steaming northward across the line of the Approach Buoys. There was something unusual about her. "Hold on, Bill," I called, and reached for my binoculars. She was flying the Danish flag. Foreigners had been suspected of mine-laying recently, so we bore away under *Ben Attow's* stern and started a long chase after the Dane that ended nearly an hour later off Arbroath. By the time we had spoken her and satisfied ourselves of her *bona fides,* the *Ben Attow* was hull down and out of mind.

We came off patrol that night and steamed up river to Dundee while I cleaned for shore to report to N.O.I.C. as usual.

He was speaking on the telephone, but waved me to a chair.

"Hold on a moment," I heard him say. "The commanding officer of one of our patrol drifters has just come in. I'll ask him." He turned to me. "Cameron and McFarlane are a bit worried about one of their trawlers. She's a day overdue apparently. I expect you know her; she's the *Ben Attow.*"

"Why, she was fishing this morning out by the Approach Buoys!"

"Are you sure?"

"Quite sure, sir. We almost went alongside for a fry."

N.O.I.C. passed the news with obvious relief. Apparently another trawler had reported an explosion during the night off the Firth of Forth where *Ben Attow* was known to be fishing.

Later that evening N.O.I.C. sent for me to produce the log.

"You must have been mistaken," he said quietly. "That couldn't have been the *Ben Attow.*"

I was completely taken aback. "But, sir," I expostulated, "we all saw her—five of us at least."

27

"Sorry, but I can only say that a trawler's wheelhouse was picked up early this morning off St. Abb's Head."

"It must have come off some other trawler, sir."

N.O.I.C. shook his head. "I'd like to think so, but, you see, the wreckage had the name *Ben Attow* on it."

I talked it over with the crew that night. They were frankly incredulous. At last Tommy Green, who was ever a man of few words, thumped on the table and stood up.

"We're a' daft. I'm awa' to ma bed."

After that it was tacitly agreed to avoid the subject.

One morning following a dirty night we went out over the Bar and came across the main beam of a vessel complete with official number. We reported our find by signal to Buddon, and learned that a ship had been sunk outside during the night. Presently we came up with a great deal of debris and the body of a woman kept afloat by voluminous black clothes. Close by we picked up a handbag containing a Latvian identity card, letters, loose change, and all the usual feminine impedimenta.

Then came a signal to search for floating mines reported by trawlers and to warn shipping that the port was closed.

Until then the war had seemed somewhat unreal and remote. But that night in the open sea, with mines around and a dead woman under a tarpaulin on the foredeck, the machinations of a jaded but none the less fertile imagination served to bring it home.

The sequel was curious. The vessel was a Latvian steamer that had struck a mine just as she was about to anchor outside to await a pilot. The dead woman, whom we had imagined from the contents of the handbag to be a stewardess, was in fact the captain's wife. The real owner of the bag got ashore through the surf with several others, and spent the night in the sand dunes. Needless to say, she was astounded to have her bag returned and celebrated her escape by marrying one of the rescued men.

Later it was rumoured that the captain's wife had hundreds of banknotes sewn inside her clothing. How much truth there was in it I do not know, but the report reaching the base that the steamer was laden with tinned ham, butter and eggs was certainly correct, for barrels and cases were floating about

for weeks, and *Venture's* crew, going off home on leave, were not empty-handed.

In the early spring a night patrol outside was established mainly for mine-watching, and steam drifters entirely manned by T-124 crews were employed. One in particular was a chummy ship of ours, and whenever we relieved each other her ever-cheerful skipper and I leaned out of our wheelhouse windows and exchanged comments on the weather and things in general while the crews indulged in verbal sallies concerning a certain mysterious and presumably mythical person of the Dundee waterfront by name Tattie Bell, much to the enjoyment of Tommy Green.

Then one evening we happened to be lying alongside each other off Buddon. There was much scuttling to and fro, and presently the skipper invited me aboard with a broad bucolic grin, but I begged to be excused as I had arrears of sleep to make up.

Two hours later I was awakened by the Chief looking at me solemnly from the doorway.

"If you're wantin' oot on patrol the nicht, you'd better git the boys back aboard."

I made to turn out, but the Chief would not hear of it. "I'll gie word to the skipper an' mate," he said, and presently there was much shouting and laughter, followed by three dull thuds.

It was the skipper's turn to grin at me.

"Are they all right, Skipper?" I asked.

"Aye. They're aboard."

An hour later we had to get under way. Ours was a towsled-headed crew that had to let go their own lines, for not a soul stirred aboard our neighbour. Whether the steam drifter ever got out that night I never heard, but the skipper must have had a great deal of explaining to the Paymaster-Commander to account for the disappearance of his medicinal comforts!

The Germans became somewhat more active off the East Coast of Scotland early in the New Year. The threatened surface attack never materialized, but there were minings, presumably by plane, for they seemed to be laid in pairs. There was machine-gunning, too, from time to time. The South Carr Light Vessel was shot up by a hit-and-run raider, and the

29

s.s. *Stancourt,* waiting outside the Bar for the fog to lift, was also attacked. She weighed and came in on her own without a pilot, only to go aground inside.

The local sweepers and drifters worked on her for nearly a month and finally got her off. Three years later I was sent for by the Paymaster at Portland and handed my share of the salvage money amounting to £21.

Another salvage job with which we were concerned in *Venture* was the motor-coaster *Crombie.* We came across her one fine sunny forenoon lying stopped off the South Carr Light Vessel and flying International Flag-F, indicating she was disabled.

The skipper wanted a signal sent to his owners in Dundee for a spare part to be sent out.

"We've no wireless aboard," I said.

The skipper shrugged his shoulders. "We're working on the engine," he replied. "If not we'll have to sail her."

The Chief was standing by me. "D'you reckon we'd get her in? " I asked.

"Ach, yes. She'd dae it richt enough."

I offered a tow, but either the skipper thought us too small for the job or wanted to avoid a salvage claim, for he just shook his head, whereupon we made off and passed a message by Aldis lamp as soon as we could raise the signal station on Buddon High Light.

Meantime, the wind was beginning to blow up from the south-west, and when we returned the laden *Crombie* was wallowing broadside on and rolling her decks under. H.M. trawler *Cranefly,* also out of Dundee, was trying to pass a hawser, and we stood by until they were fairly under way. By that time there was a heavy sea running, and we could be of no further assistance, so we left them and returned to harbour. That night it came on to blow a full gale, and we were glad to be in. *Cranefly* and *Crombie* parted the towline several times, and once during the night they all but piled up on the Bell Rock. Eventually they made port the following afternoon.

Coming in from sea with the wind easterly, we sometimes had to wait outside for the ebb to slacken. There was always the risk of being pooped and of broaching to, yet to leave it too late after dark was even more frightening. I took the wheel

on these occasions, as I felt the responsibility was mine. Once started, there was no turning back, and it was a comfort to have the Chief murmuring out of the corner of his mouth so that none but I could hear.

"She's seen mair sea than this at the fishin'. Ach! Jist gie it tae her full belt. She'll dae it a'richt."

A few moments to secure everything on deck; a shout of warning to the cook, and we were away.

Soon there would come the lift as a sea caught up with us, driving us on, then tossing us up and rolling from under away out ahead. And again the hiss and roar heralding a crested roller, and again that almost irresistible urge to glance astern at that towering, curling wall of water that threatened to break and poop us. Then again that fiercely thrilling scend and surge as we swept along, fighting, heaving, sweating at the wheel.

On the whole we were lucky with the weather that winter in spite of the cold spell that froze the River Tay. Only once were we really caught out at sea. Then we made to come in over the Bar at slack water, but hove-to instead to watch one of the trawlers essay the passage. She tossed about amid the combers and disappeared into the murk. Perhaps we could have done it, but I decided to run for shelter in the Firth of Forth, where we put into St. Monance, which is surely one of the prettiest fishing villages in Britain.

On another occasion we were waiting for our relief at dusk. All day the wind had been easterly and freshening. Presently we saw the steam drifter making her way out, pitching and rolling. Visibility was bad, and she seemed an unconscionably long time. Then she started to flash us. We were both jumping about, and we only read a word here and there.

"Something aboot man overboard," said the mate.

"That's what I thought, but she's still coming out."

We made over towards her. The wheelhouse windows were smashed; whole sections of the bulwarks were missing, and the skipper had blood pouring down his face.

"We lost two men overboard on the Bar," he shouted. "Picked up one, but lost the other. We're flooded out down below."

Normally we would have waited for the ebb to slacken;

light was fading though, and soon it would be impossible to see anybody in the water at all.

I decided to have a try. "Where did you say it was?"

The skipper gave us the position. "Watch yourself," he cautioned. "There's a wicked sea running."

We saw no sign of life on the Bar. Nobody could have lived in that sea; I doubt whether we could have rounded up, anyway.

"Is there anything more we can do?" I asked the crew. They shuffled their feet and shook their heads.

A little later that night we received orders to proceed to Dundee. My appointment had just come through to Captain M.L.'s Staff at Portsmouth, for the newly formed Coastal Forces.

CHAPTER IV

COASTAL FORCES

M.L. 1031 was built at Lymington—the first of the 72-ft. diesel-engined motor launches—and assigned to Captain M.L., Portsmouth, for training duties.

Trials were amusing. We had come round to Haslar Creek for stores and ammunition; the Admiralty constructor arrived with his party, and realized we were going to be deeper than our designed draft, whereupon he ordered the removal of four depth charges. He also stopped coxswain from taking aboard fresh water. Then, with twenty officials scattered about the decks, we put to sea. It was blowing hard south-west; we rolled in the beam sea, and our visitors hurriedly clutched at the hand rails. We rounded Horse Sand Fort and headed into wind and sea. Spray flew over the ship, and the wheelhouse was soon crammed with a reeling, reeking mass of humanity.

There was too much sea running in Stokes Bay for measured mile trials. We tried Cowes, but the constructor was still not satisfied, and eventually we found reasonably quiet conditions in Southampton Water. After the usual turning and astern trials we made for home. The designer took the wheel, consistently over-steering as she yawed and rolled, while the rest of the party packed like sardines into wheelhouse and ward-room.

" Can you manage tea for everyone, Cox'n? " I asked.

" Sorry, sir," he replied. " No water, sir."

" What, none at all? " gasped the sweating helmsman.

" No, sir. Orders not to water ship, sir! "

These 72-ft. M.L.s, with their sweet, round-bilge hull form, would have shown a better turn of speed with another ten feet on their stern and quarters filled out, for they tended to suck down at ten knots, and twelve knots was about their maximum. Doubtless the designer was aware of this, for tank tests had proved that a third engine would only have given an extra knot and no more, and the limitation of length was imposed by

considerations of transport as deck cargo overseas. With a range of 2,500 miles, though, these Harbour Defence M.L.s, as they came to be known, later made excellent ocean passages under their own power.

Shortly afterwards H.M.S. *St. Christopher* was established at Fort William to train Coastal Force personnel, and we made the trip round to the West Coast of Scotland. It was midwinter, but *1031* found the long seas of the Western Approaches to her liking. She was still inclined to throw spray about as she knocked the top off a sea, but with her stern freed, she averaged twelve knots whatever the weather.

It was a cold trip through the Irish Sea. We made Larne at dusk in a snowstorm. Next day we caught a pasting off the Mull of Kintyre and steamed up the Firth of Lorne and Loch Linnhe, cold and somewhat awed by the desolate, snow-bound grandeur of the Highlands, and marvelling at the hardiness of the Scots in their tiny remote crofts at the foot of the hills.

It was unusual, so we were told, for the weather to be so severe. Nor was our reception in the mess much warmer, although the commander was affable enough. I had volunteered for service in the Mediterranean, but he asked me to stay on with the Training Flotilla for six weeks or so. Then he offered me a sherry and introduced me to some of the base staff.

" I take it, sir, we're allowed to use the mess when we come ashore? " I asked.

The commander turned to his chief training officer. "That's all right, I suppose? "

" Why, yes," came the reply in a supercilious drawl. " So long as he doesn't come too often."

The next day was Sunday. We lay in Camus-na-Gall on the far side of the loch. I took a saw and an axe ashore to spend the day woodcutting and felt better afterwards.

There were too many wars being waged in *St. Christopher* in those early days, but we of the Training Flotilla found it possible to steer clear of most of them by keeping to ourselves. It was not always comfortable or convenient, but at least it was peaceful. The ratings under training were volunteers from the Fleet for the most part, and there was little we could teach them. The officers were from trawlers, armed yachts and armed merchant cruisers. They knew far more than I of the Navy;

34

all they wanted was the opportunity of handling Coastal Force craft.

Officers under training were inclined to be somewhat high-spirited ashore, and sometimes jibbed at the irksome discipline. One day, while my first lieutenant was away on leave, a signal came off that an officer was being sent to me for a week, and that he was to be allowed neither shore leave nor wine account. To my surprise a strapping young Canadian with twinkling eyes came aboard. Apparently there had been a farewell party the previous night, so Bill told me. The first lieutenant of the base went upstairs to stop the row, and was greeted with a bucket of water that was really intended for another. This sobered them somewhat, and they were persuaded to go to their cabins. Bill turned in, but some of the others raided him with sand and water from the fire buckets.

"What happened? Why, one of the Wrens complained next morning, and I went up before the captain. The others were going on to *Sea Hawk* for their A/S course, and I didn't want them to get pipped."

"So you took the can back?" I said.

"I guess I did." Then Bill grinned. "You know, I never drank back home. Gee! That's mighty strong stuff, that Highland whisky!"

Bill was a grand chap and took a keen interest in the training. Three food parcels arrived for him during the week, the last containing the most luxurious cake I have ever tasted. It bore the label of the Toronto Bible Society.

"They must know you of old, Bill."

"Well," he replied with some diffidence, "as a matter of fact I'm president of the society!"

My original spell of six weeks in the Training Flotilla became prolonged indefinitely. Towards the middle of 1941 we went through the Caledonian Canal to refit at Inverness. The countryside was magnificent and the canal banks a blaze of yellow gorse. Dorothy came north. Inverness was full and hotel accommodation difficult to obtain; eventually we were lent a houseboat in Dochfours—one of the most beautiful natural parts of the Canal—close by Bona Light at the eastern end of Loch Ness. The boat belonged to the medical superintendent of the mental hospital, and came from the White Star

35

liner *Olympic,* broken up at Inverkeithing. The doctor had
it towed round to Inverness by fishermen relatives of one of
the patients, and handed it over for conversion to an old ship-
wright inmate as a form of occupational therapy. It was a
most successful treatment, for not only did he recover his
reason, but—so the story goes—sent in his bill!

The weather was superb. For water we simply dipped overside, and, having borrowed cycles, we were independent of
the somewhat spasmodic bus service. One evening we went
to the Islands at Inverness to hear the pipe band of the
Cameron Highlanders, and, coming back along the canal
bank towards midnight, found to our astonishment the auxiliary
Thames sailing barge *Hydrogen* moored by Bona Light. We
pulled round her entranced. It was still broad daylight, but
her crew were turned in and we reluctantly left, with the intention of speaking her next morning. But alas! she was gone
when I looked out at six o'clock.

Apparently *Hydrogen* was on passage to the Clyde, where
several auxiliary barges found employment during the war.

When *1031* went away to Lowestoft to carry out training of
Patrol Service ratings, I was appointed to another ship of the
Training Flotilla, the Fairmile B-type *M.L. 269,* built at
Cockenzie in the Firth of Forth. These twin-screw 112-ft. craft
had American 87-octane petrol engines, and were capable of
bursts of up to twenty-one knots. They were partially prefabri-
cated and built at yacht yards all round the coast, with an
easily driven, round-bilge hull, and good accommodation that
made them very popular craft. They were easily handled and
magnificent sea boats, well suited for our job, as it was possible
now to have both officers and men aboard for training.

When *269* went for a long refit I was appointed to *M.L. 485,*
built down in Essex by Cardnell Brothers in the true family
tradition, miles away from anywhere. Mr. G. E. Cardnell
built yachts at Steeple for many years, and carted them across
fields to the nearest water; now his two sons had put up a fine
shed at Maylandsea and were turning out first-rate craft.

M.L. 485 was copper-bottomed, and later sailed to the West
Indies, but I left her at Great Yarmouth with my ribs stove
in from a soccer match against one of the local-based M.G.B.s.

Some weeks later I found myself in *M.L. 490*, built by Curtis, of Looe, and back again once more in the Training Flotilla.

I had learnt many things commissioning *485*. I had seen for myself how green were the crews of the newly commissioned Coastal Force craft. Nor was it to be wondered at, for officers were now coming direct from H.M.S. *King Alfred*, and ratings were " Hostilities Only " and new entries at that. It was evident to me that our system of training at *St. Christopher* was inadequate, and, having time on my hands lying around with a strapped chest, I worked out a scheme whereby each craft of the Training Flotilla might be manned by a skeleton, hand-picked, permanent crew, and made up to complement with trainees.

The more I reflected on the idea, the better I liked it. I submitted my report with great enthusiasm, but it was too revolutionary and crossed too many people's bows. It was turned down, and I thereupon decided it was time to get back to operational service. My request was passed on by the captain with his blessing. That, too, was turned down by the Admiralty, whose reply, " *He appears to be eminently suited to his present appointment and must stay where he is,*" was ironical but final. There was no alternative but to make the best of the training job with all its limitations. Luckily, Dorothy found a small furnished cottage on the hillside, and settled in with Elizabeth, our wartime baby.

Life was really quite good in spite of a natural feeling of frustration. In due course I even found myself senior officer with a half-stripe. The Flotilla grew in numbers until we had seventeen M.L.s, apart from gunboats and M.T.B.s. It was a good flotilla and the craft were well looked after, even though refits were few and far between. Commanding officers and first lieutenants were the best that could be found for the job. Many were pre-war sailing men. Operational experience was not the essential qualification; rather was it a natural aptitude coupled with enthusiasm and capacity for hard work. It was certainly no sinecure, as the older officers who were appointed at an earlier stage soon discovered.

One of these old-timers had to proceed into Fort William from the moorings opposite Corpach. He was inside boat, and elected to swing between the trot and the shore. He got athwart

the tide and was creeping ahead when those of us taking the air on deck that quiet Sunday morning were amazed to hear the order: "Slow ahead together."

"Slow ahead together, sir?" repeated the coxswain in a note of pained surprise.

The commanding officer showed signs of anxiety, as well he might, for unless he went astern quickly there was a collision in the offing.

"Half ahead, together!"

"Half ahead, sir?" screamed the thoroughly startled coxswain.

"That's right. Half ahead—full ahead!"

There was no time for the coxswain to reply. The sharp clipper bows were already cutting into the other M.L.'s engine room.

At last the full-time training in the Flotilla did come about. It had to; it was indeed the only logical method. Ratings and officers continued to train both ashore and afloat for three weeks, then for their last week they joined the Flotilla as part of the ship's company. We were crowded in the wardroom as well as on the messdeck, but we were happy ships, and each of the permanent crew took his share in training duties. We were too busy for much painting, nor was Fort William weather conducive, but the M.L.s were the cleanest and best kept of any in Coastal Forces. The enthusiasm of the new entries for their first ship was a joy to behold, and they never failed to impress coxswain with their appetites.

We trained in the waters of Loch Linnhe, with an extended cruise to the Western Isles every fourth week. Each new crew was handed over to the first lieutenant and subjected to a furious crescendo of practical training.

One day, towards the end of the week's work, we put into Cul Bay. The first lieutenant had his party on the foredeck. The leadsman was taking soundings and singing out in the approved manner; the signalman was standing by to hoist church pendant; another had the black ball handy. We were to anchor, rig side-ladder and away dinghy.

"Deep four, sir. . . . And a half three!"

"Stop engines."

"By the mark three."

"Slow astern together."

"Ship going astern, sir."

"Stop engines. Let go! "

The first lieutenant galvanized into life. "Off brake," he yelled.

The chain ran out. Unnoticed, the lad at the windlass still slacked away at his brake handle. Then the first lieutenant began to make furious signs. In desperation he tried to check the chain by jumping on it. I rang slow ahead, but it was too late. The chain gathered momentum. Suddenly there was silence and the first lieutenant turned to me biting his nails, half sardonic, half apologetic smile on his face. The man at the windlass stood gaping at the brake handle in his hand. The rest gazed dejectedly at the bubbles under the bows.

We never did recover that anchor and chain.

Those were full, happy days at Fort William during 1943, when thousands of officers and ratings passed through *St. Christopher*. Their training ashore was enlightened and calculated to kindle enthusiasm, so that when they came afloat to work ship, it was a sheer joy to have them. They left to join their operational craft on the crest of a wave; there was no gainsaying that the morale of Coastal Forces during the strenuous months that followed was exceedingly high.

We had our flashes of humour, too. *M.L. 167* was leaking aft, and the commanding officer made a signal to the base and repeated to me as senior officer:

St. Christopher (R) S.O.M.L. from M.L. 167.
Am making twelve inches of water daily in Wardroom Flat.
02/1545

It was too good an opportunity to miss, and I hurriedly sent off a signal which was duly distributed through the S.D.O. as follows: —

M.L. 167 (R) St. Christopher, all M.L.s from S.O.M.L.
Your 02/1545 addressed St. Christopher. This practice must cease forthwith. *02/1830*
Ref. making water in W/R Flat.

A few days later, when the story had gone the rounds, the captain sent for me. It was business at first, then just as I was leaving he cleared his throat and looked down his nose.

39

"About that signal———"

I waited for the storm.

"Hmm. I saw it in the signal log the other day," then his face relaxed and a twinkle came into his eye. "Very funny. Most humorous."

Which recalls the commanding officer of *H.D.M.L. 1049*, who made a signal to the medical officer, calling attention to morning sickness among his crew. The M.O. in his reply rather suspected poor ventilation, but suggested a search just in case there was a man aboard!

*   *   *   *   *

Early in 1944 I suddenly found myself in Combined Operations in command of the new Itchenor-built *M.L. 594* and senior officer of the 7th M.L. Flotilla. There were twelve of us attached to Force G as navigational leaders to the assault craft. The gear we carried was something of a nightmare, for we had radar, echo-sounder, Q.H. (as we knew the Bomber Command "Gee" set, forerunner of the Decca navigator), anti-submarine equipment, Chernikeef log, and several wireless sets. We were armed with Oerlikons in addition to the usual 3-pounder, twin-Vickers and depth charges. Specialist ratings brought our complement to twenty-five, and we carried a junior navigating officer.

Apart from the customary teething troubles and shaking down, the main problem was to get acclimatized to the atmosphere of Combined Operations. The multiplicity of types of craft was bewildering. I never did manage to comprehend all the abbreviations, but tank landing craft were known as L.C.T., and the smaller, box-like L.C.A. carried the assault troops; they were the craft we came to know best.

We were too late forming up as a flotilla to take part in more than two of the exercises, but the memory of "Fabius" will ever haunt my dreams. Sailing out from the Solent by way of the Needles Channel, round the Isle of Wight, and assaulting at first light on the beaches of Hayling Island, we realized later that conditions had been made to simulate the Normandy landing as much as possible.

Our special task was to lead in the first wave of assault craft. If we stopped and fell off, as an M.L. will, they immediately re-formed astern. The navigation was the least of our troubles.

It was the aftermath that was so appalling, the sorting out, marshalling, carrying orders, passing signals to craft we failed to recognize. The loud-hailer failed; signals became incomprehensible; we were utterly tired out and dispirited. Then came instructions to return thirteen L.C.T.s to harbour and TURCO them, which meant reporting them, together with lists of defects, stores requirements, etc. Away we went to their anchorage. We hailed, bullied and cajoled. Some weighed anchor; others failed to respond. Eventually we set course for the Spithead Gate and the raggle-taggle procession somehow formed into line. By the time we were off Cowes we had landing craft following astern in perfect formation as far as the eye could see. Which were our thirteen I had not the faintest notion. In desperation I left them to make their own way up Southampton Water, while we doubled back to Portsmouth. We counted up to sixty-six, and they were still streaming through the Gate.

A few days later we had our L.C.A. Flotilla officers aboard for lunch. They were seasoned veterans of Sicily and Salerno, and we told them something of our troubles.

" You reckon you'll be able to lead us in all right, though? "

" Good Lord, yes. We're not concerned about that end of the business. It's just that we're not used to combined ops."

They shrugged their shoulders. So long as we landed them on the right beach at the right time, what else was there to worry about? We relaxed and enjoyed ourselves.

Towards the end of May it became obvious that D-Day was not far off. The London Symphony Orchestra came to the Southampton Guildhall and gave a superb performance of Beethoven's Fifth to a crowded house. A few days later I was there again for briefing. Elaborate security measures were enforced; identity cards were scrutinized; the doors were locked —so we were told. The naval commander Force G—a slim, impressive figure—had just started on his introductory remarks when it became apparent that officers were filtering into the hall.

N.C. Force G stopped short. "Who are you chaps? " he demanded, as staff officers jumped down from the platform and hurried to the back of the hall to investigate.

" We're from the destroyers, sir," came the reply. "We had engine trouble coming ashore."

"Who let you in?"

"We just came through the door, sir!"

N.C. Force G. shrugged his shoulders. So much for the vaunted security! The tension broke with a roar of laughter.

I came away from the briefing haunted by a secret—the secret of the Normandy invasion that Germans would have given much to possess. I knew it; so did thousands more, and it seemed that to achieve complete surprise was beyond the bounds of possibility.

Then came the bright, sunny day when *Bulolo,* our headquarters ship, sailed down Southampton Water, while we of the 7th M.L. Flotilla followed astern, playing over the loudhailer what we called the navigational leaders' theme song: "*We don't know where we're going till we're there.*"

The craft that packed the Solent began to put to sea. It was dark when we sailed out through the Needles Channel, still dancing attendance on *Bulolo* and the L.S.I.s—landing ships infantry—carrying our assault craft in davits. Planes droned overhead. All through the night we were overtaking slower craft, and some of the smaller ones were making heavy weather of it. Then just before dawn the L.S.I.s brought up and lowered away. We stood off and hoisted a dim blue light. The L.C.A.s formed up astern, and we moved off at a steady four knots, creeping in towards the shore.

We were keyed up—tense—silent. It was beginning to come light. Presently the first lieutenant emerged from the wheelhouse, where he and the navigator had been busy on the charts. He gazed around, then grinned and made to drop below.

"What's bitten you, Number One?"

"I was just thinking, sir, of old Jerry ashore there coming out for a stretch and a yawn, then suddenly catching sight of all us lot. Christ!"

"Hundreds an' thousands of 'em!" added the Cockney signalman.

"Bet his old eyes don't half pop out," said coxswain.

We began to chuckle. Then we roared with laughter, prolonging that blessed sense of relief until we clung helpless to the wings of the bridge. In some mysterious fashion the joke spread to the guns' crews; steel helmets met in conclave, then tilted back in a burst of guffaws.

Soon we were taking station on the L.C.T.s with AVREs aboard—tanks fitted with every device for easing the path of our assault forces. The air bombardment was on. Then came broadsides from the battleships. It was light now, and the coast loomed up. Self-propelled guns in L.C.T.s opened up as they came in. L.C.F.s and L.C.G.s (flakboats and gunboats) joined in with close-support fire. We started a programme of music over the loud-hailer. Then up went the rockets from the rocketeers on either bow, obliterating the quiet, unpretentious beach of Le Hamel. Shortly afterwards the L.C.R.s on the flanks fired. Their rockets soared lazily into the sky, and it seemed they could never reach the beach. Yet they did, and up went more smoke and dust. The uplift to morale was tremendous, for nothing could possibly survive on the beaches, so it seemed to us.

Our L.C.A.s deployed.

"Ten feet," sung out the navigating officer as he watched the echo-sounder. "Shoaling all the time, sir."

Shells dropped close ahead.

We made to the flotilla officers: *All yours. Good luck.* The L.C.A.s revved up. We stopped and they came on past, the troops in good heart, squatting on their haunches, with netting over their steel helmets.

"Aren't you coming in with us? " one of them shouted.

We grinned and gave them a cheer. The L.C.A.s scurried for the shore, with white wakes showing up for all the world like rabbits' scuts.

We watched them beach with a curious mixture of elation and anti-climax. The next L.C.A.s came in, followed by wave after wave of landing craft. The Baie de la Seine at least was ours.

During the days that followed we maintained ourselves as best we could, scrounging stores, chasing mail, picking up cases of American K rations out of the water, maintaining A/S patrol by day, making smoke by night during each inevitable air attack, taking in landing craft to the beaches, salvaging derelicts, passing orders, escorting craft halfway across the Channel, dodging the weather as best we could, dragging our anchor in the poor holding ground, and all the time growing more and more weary and unkempt.

Tugs came in with massive concrete sections for the Mulberry Harbour, great convoys of merchant ships and L.S.T.s, all manner of landing craft and transports, even Thames lighters fitted out as floating galleys with batteries of tall smoke stacks. Tanks and vehicles and troops and stores poured ashore. This was the great build-up. We lived those days in a dream of wonderment.

Petrol was a problem until we finally located a converted Thames lighter close in by the beach displaying a board: *87 OCTANE.* The skipper was a cheery Patrol Service petty officer whose speech proclaimed his identity as a lighterman in spite of naval uniform. He had made the crossing in bad weather under his own power, with only a vague idea of the position of the British beaches. There was no stove on board. To cook a meal, they started up one of the engines and heated cans on the exhaust pipe that led aft on deck. It was a strange berth for a Thames lighter with high octane petrol aboard. Not that our lighterman cared.

"We're all right, gov'nor. Got a grandstand view of the fireworks an' all!"

Then there was the small water tanker anchored well inshore. We were their first customer, so the skipper said. He had come over to the assault area early on, and asked for instructions.

"They just said to go inshore as far as I liked and anchor. So we did. That was three days ago, and nobody's been near since."

"Do you want us to pass a signal about you?" I asked.

"No, no, sir. We're quite happy. Plenty to eat—and drink!" he added with a smile. "Running a bit low on baccy, though, that's all."

We let them have what we could and came away. Theirs was the typical philosophical outlook of the Merchant Navy. There was no hurry so far as they were concerned. When their tanks were empty they would only go back for more.

With so much going alongside in the open roadstead we were soon desperately short of lines and fenders, and tried to enlist the sympathy of the cruiser *Frobisher,* but the officer of the watch shook his head and waved us away, whereupon

my first lieutenant assumed a lugubrious expression and crooned through the loud-hailer a soulful rendering of—

> "*I ain't nobody's darling,*
> *Nobody loves me . . ."*

There were broad grins aboard the *Frobisher*. The officer of the watch disappeared for a few moments, then hailed us to come alongside. He was a South African and a grand chap. My first lieutenant went off with their commissioned boatswain and presently sang out for a couple of hands; coxswain stepped aboard armed with chits and came back well loaded with bread and meat; I followed later with bath towel and soap. She was a fine ship, *Frobisher*.

After three weeks we were badly in need of maintenance. At last our relief arrived and we set off for Portsmouth, escorting L.C.T.s. H.M.S. *Hornet,* the Coastal Force base in Haslar Creek, took us in hand with magnificent efficiency, but what really surprised us was the seventy-two hours' leave the captain gave us.

That same night I took the train north. We were late at Edinburgh and I travelled on to Fort William by the Oban line, changing at Connel Ferry and creeping round the Lochs to Ballachulish. The ferry was over on the other side of the Narrows, with Dorothy and Elizabeth just clambering aboard.

"Daddy, *Daddy,* DADDY! " Elizabeth screamed in a perfect frenzy of delight, and all the way across she was dancing about, and I could hear her telling everybody, "That's my Daddy. That's my Daddy."

It is curious how such little things make everything well worth while.

CHAPTER V

TROUT LINE

ON the way back to the ship I called to see my mother in South-East London, a great gardener, who soon had me trotting round looking at her flowers. Presently came an ominous, grinding rumble. I looked up, but the clouds were low and I could see nothing.

"Don't worry about that. It's a buzz bomb passing over Chislehurst way," she assured me.

There came a distant explosion; my collar felt a little tight about my neck.

"Now come and see my currants. Oh, that's all right," she added as there came another crackling rumble. "That's coming up the Thames. Now, did you ever see such lovely black currants?"

This was my first acquaintance with flying bombs, and I found them disquieting. Presently mother looked up and listened.

"Perhaps we'd better go in for a few moments. This one's coming over our way."

It was low, too. The engine seemed to falter. Then suddenly it cut right out, and I felt myself coming out in a cold sweat.

But mother was not in the least perturbed. "It's gone over," she said quietly, and we waited for the loud explosion, Lewisham way.

It was a relief to get back to the Normandy shore, where the defence had been reorganized and the 7th M.L. Flotilla allocated to work with the Support Squadron on the eastern flank, which was still under sporadic fire from the guns beyond the River Orne.

Each evening we sailed out from the anchorage, with Frank Sinatra and his heavenly choir crooning "*What a lovely way to spend an evening*" over the loud-hailer, to man Trout Line, as we called the eastern limit of the assault area. The L.C.F.s

and L.C.G.s anchored, while we M.L.s maintained anti-submarine patrol and radar watch.

Every night there was an air attack lasting about two hours, then it usually quietened down to an uneasy calm. Some-times there were battles going on between Light Forces away to the south-east, with green and red tracer criss-crossing low down on the horizon. Then that would end abruptly and the hours strung out until dawn.

One night we lay astern of an L.C.G. The nightly flap was over. For an hour or more we stood around on the bridge.

At last I broke the silence. "Go on, Number One. Turn in for a couple of hours."

The first lieutenant bestirred himself. "I'm all right, sir. Why don't you take a spell?"

Another ten minutes passed. All was quiet. Against my better judgment I allowed myself to be persuaded and went aft to the wardroom and lay down on the settee.

Suddenly I woke to a terrific clatter from the twin Oerlikons directly overhead, and found myself on the deck entangled in the dark with the tablecloth. I groped my way to the door-way, and, still completely bewildered, fought with the double blackout curtains, finally to emerge in the flat with the night turned to day. I grabbed my steel helmet and crept on deck. Strings of flares hung in the sky; I felt as naked as the day I was born.

A string of bombs came whistling down. Ducking and crawling past the Oerlikons, I made my way to the bridge, my knees as weak as water, and there I propped myself in my corner, while the first lieutenant carried on with his job of fire control. He was far too busy to take any notice of me. One by one the flares went out. The racket died down. Then he turned to me with a rueful smile.

"Sorry, sir, but I didn't have a chance to call you out. Jerry properly caught us on the hop."

It was fully half an hour before I recovered my wits. There-after, on Trout Line, I never left the bridge; one experience was enough of that terrifying, unnerving, paralytic fear that saps all strength from the body and stifles initiative and thought.

Those patrols were seldom dull. An M.L. reported having

sighted a curious whitish blob drifting by in the dark, which failed to register on A/S or radar. The following night, having had our nightly strafe, we were again lying astern of an L.C.G., when they hailed us to say a couple of blobs had drifted along their side and they were unable to bring their light guns to bear. We slipped, but found nothing, and went away down tide to come back dropping depth charges. Then we learned that yet another had come past, which the L.C.G. had sunk with small arms, capturing the one-man crew. The blobs were the perspex domes of human torpedoes—one torpedo-like craft with a real one slung beneath.

They were launched from Dives-Houlgate during the night and came filtering through Trout Line on the ebb, with the intention of attacking ships in the anchorage. Very few of them got through; even fewer found their way back on the flood. Out of seventy or more that set out that night less than ten returned, so we heard later.

Then came the pick-a-back planes, the lower one filled with explosives and released from a shallow dive to come skidding across the water with a great noise and a stream of sparks.

Another night we heard a plane coming out from the land. It was low—very low—but we could see nothing of her until she was right on top of us. She must have spotted us at the very last moment, for she wheeled away and her wing just cleared our mast. It was then we saw she was German. An L.C.F. opened fire. A few seconds later we heard a splash. There was no explosion; just complete silence. We made over towards it; two or three cables to the eastward there was a great stench of petrol, but it was very dark and we found nothing.

Each morning we returned to the anchorage, playing the other side of our Frank Sinatra record:

> " *I never slept a wink last night.*
> *Why did we have that silly fight?* "

Two M.L.s each day steamed off for stores and mail; the rest of us anchored to shoreward of our headquarters ship, the China River gunboat *Locust*. We had breakfast, followed by a general clear up, then piped down. It was sleep we coveted

more than anything; a whole night in was our idea of heavenly bliss.

We obtained permission one afternoon to land a party in search of fresh vegetables, and picked our way between the wrecks into the Gooseberry, as the abandoned harbour of old sunken ships was called. Leaving the navigator in command, with one part of a watch, the rest of us went ashore in a DUCKW, and, having been warned to keep away from un-cleared houses, we strolled along a lane towards Luc-sur-Mer —a welcome change from our cramped decks. Presently we came to a small market garden and a villa set back from the road, with a shell hole in the roof. A lady was loading a small cart with vegetables.

Coxswain nudged me. " Go on, sir. She's got just the sort of stuff we want—onions an' all. Ask her how much."

With some diffidence, for the lady's appearance was.somewhat intimidating, I walked up the little drive and saluted.

" Good afternoon, Madame," I said in my best French. " Have you any vegetables for sale? "

" But yes." It seemed she was just off to the market at Caen. What did we wish? She named a price for onions, which I passed to Coxswain, who did a rapid calculation and looked down his nose.

" Sounds a bit dear to me, sir," he said. " Still, we'd better have it, I suppose," and he called to a rating with an empty sack to come up. " I've got a bit of soap here if it's any use to her," and pulled out a bar of " Pusser's Hard."

Madame stood literally transfixed. She could hardly believe her eyes, and when Coxswain held it out her hands trembled.

" C'est pour moi? " she exclaimed. " Oh, monsieur! " Her hands made an expressive gesture over her dress. " Oh, je suis complètement sale. But now . . ."

Coxswain brought out a tablet of toilet soap. It was more than she could bear. Tears came into her eyes as she held it against her face. The years seemed to drop from her; she was no longer the forbidding woman we had supposed, but an attractive person of forty-two or three. She told me, with a wealth of gesture, of life in France during the occupation; how that June morning, when we were bolstering our morale by chuckling at the thought of taking the Germans by surprise,

49

she was actually on the way to the station and soldiers came rushing past crying out: "*Achtung! Achtung!* The English are here! " And when the shells started to come over she and her family had taken refuge in a ditch until presently German soldiers retreating across her field had been shot down in the far corner.

" *Ils étaient toujours correctes, les Allemands.*" Then, with an expressive shrug: " One did not love them, of course, but one got accustomed to having them about."

The momentary sadness passed. Madame's face lit up again; there was animated beauty in her smile as she swept the vegetables into the sacks and refused to take any money. She had the soap. That sufficed.

But Coxswain was perplexed. "That's not right, sir," he protested. "We can't take all that lot just for a bit of soap," and he produced tea and canned meat, while the crew had a whip round for cigarettes.

We left her speechless, her arms full, smiling through her tears. The Germans started shelling us on the way back.

One night the commander of the Support Squadron Eastern Flank (S.S.E.F.) himself came with us on patrol. Intelligence reports suggested a final sally by the Germans in the early hours of the morning with everything they had—human torpedoes, explosive motor-boats, midget submarines. At first conditions were ideal, but the weather gradually deteriorated after midnight until it seemed we were likely to be disappointed. Then a voice sang out from the A/S set:

"Echo, sir! "

I slipped on the headphones and went through the drill to bring it ahead on the bow oscillator. It was a good ping—clear and distinct—quite possibly a wreck, yet the angle of target was small.

"Slight doppler high, sir," said the A/S rating. Yes, the echo seemed slightly higher, betokening movement towards us, unless the tide was playing tricks.

I listened for a few moments, then dropped into the wheelhouse and watched the trace on the recorder.

"Bridge! " I called through the voice-pipe.

The first lieutenant answered.

"Make a signal by R/T: *Investigating contact.* Better warn the engine-room, then stand by for a pattern of three."

We closed in at half speed, then increased to fifteen knots for the attack.

"Stand by! Fire one . . . fire two . . . fire three."

We flexed our knees and waited. Three explosions hammered the hull in succession.

"Slow ahead together. Hard aport! "

We heeled and swung round, but before we regained contact, the A/S rating picked up another echo away to the southward. We steadied and held it.

"Anything on the radar at eight hundred dead ahead? "

"No, sir. Nothing on the screen."

There was no time for cautious investigation. Better go straight in to the attack.

"Full ahead together. Stand by depth charges. Fire one . . . two . . . three."

Again the jolting explosions. I rang down slow ahead, then threw off the headphones and dashed out of the wheelhouse to be met by a shout from a somewhat agitated first lieutenant.

"We've dropped a fourth," he began, when up it went. The noise was shattering. The decks heaved, and there was a sound of breaking glass below and curses from the W/T office. A great column of water rose under our very stern.

"Any more? " asked S.S.E.F. quietly.

"That's the lot, sir," replied the first lieutenant ruefully, picking himself up off the deck and rubbing his elbow.

It was too dark to see anything. We cruised around for a while, but never regained contact. The track on the iodized recorder paper looked good. But even that faded. It meant nothing, anyway, for the neighbourhood was strewn with wrecks. The rest of the night passed without further incident.

Soon afterwards we returned to England. The Flotilla were being reorganized, and *594* was to become senior officer's ship of the newly formed 13th Flotilla for service in the Burma campaign. We lay at H.M.S. *Hornet* in Haslar Creek awaiting orders to sail for Milford Haven to fit out with deck tanks, and with a view to getting away on foreign service leave as soon as possible, we handed in all surplus gear and stores.

Then Staff Officer Operations sent for me. He was short of

an M.L. for the midnight despatch boat run to Arromanches. He proposed putting us in for it and sail us on our return for Milford Haven, so that evening we berthed at Whale Island and took aboard a number of sacks. Just before midnight an R.N. captain and two very senior Army officers came aboard and were duly bedded down in the wardroom. Then, at the last moment, S.S.E.F. himself appeared.

" Good heavens! " he exclaimed. " What on earth are you doing on this run? "

I told him what was in the wind.

" I see. And how does that suit you? "

I had no hankering after Burma, but the appointment did not rest with me. In the Navy one does as one is told. I merely shrugged my shoulders and S.S.E.F. smiled.

There was quite a lop outside, but as soon as we were clear of the Gate, we increased to our maximum continuous speed of seventeen knots. We had to drive her to make Arromanches by 7 a.m.

Presently S.S.E.F. went below. The first lieutenant turned in, too, leaving me with the signalman on the bridge and the navigator in the wheelhouse calling up a fresh course from time to time. But the Channel out past the Nab was well lit, and the buoys came up like clockwork. We dodged through the shipping in the vicinity of Z Buoy, where all the South Coast and cross-Channel routes converged—Piccadilly Circus we called it—and set course for Arromanches. It began to drizzle; visibility was closing in.

I had just sung out to the navigator asking for the character of the next buoy, when the signalman spotted it.

" There it is, sir. Fine on the port bow."

" Thank you. Plot! What's the next buoy? "

There was silence for a few moments, then the navigator came out from the wheelhouse and looked around.

" Everything all right? " I asked.

" Same course, sir," he replied, and disappeared again. But I felt uneasy, with a presentiment that something was wrong. Bidding the signalman keep a good lookout, I slipped into the wheelhouse to take a look at the chart, a thing I was always loth to do at night, as it took time to get accustomed to the

dark again. On the table was a scruffy, small-scale chart I had never seen before.

"That's no good to work with," I said disgustedly. "Get yourself a decent chart out."

The navigator looked somewhat shaken. "I'm afraid that's all I've got, sir."

"Don't talk tripe. You want the continuation of the one you had just now coming out of Spithead."

"That was one I kept for the trip round to Milford Haven. I'm afraid I returned all the rest. This one was stuck at the back of the drawer."

"Good God!" I looked at the chart more closely. It was out of date and practically useless, with only a few of the Channel buoys inserted in pencil. "You'd better get the engine-room to start up the Q.H. motor. We can at least find out where we are."

"I've returned the Q.H. charts, too, sir," he replied, looking the picture of misery.

"Notices to Mariners gone as well, I suppose?"

One look at his face told me.

I shook my head in desperation, and went out on the bridge again.

"Signalman."

"Sir!"

"Give the first lieutenant a shake. Don't wake the others if you can help it."

"Aye, aye, sir."

There was another buoy flashing on the port bow, which I failed to recognize. I had a horrible feeling we were not in the Arromanches channel at all, but on the way to Cherbourg.

The signalman returned, and propped himself in the far corner.

"Just coming up, sir."

"Thank you."

A few moments later the first lieutenant swung on to the bridge.

"Anything wrong, sir?"

"Anything wrong!" I exclaimed. "Only that we're out in the middle of the Channel without any charts."

"Why, whatever's happened to them?"

53

"They've been returned, so the navigator says."

The full realization dawned on him. "My God! So they have," and he clapped his fingers to his mouth.

He went into the wheelhouse for a few moments, then came out again and stood quietly by my side. Suddenly he turned to me.

"My old navigator's note-book," he murmured. "If I haven't thrown it out, has got the courses jotted down from the last trip." He dashed aft, and returned with a grin on his face as he made for the wheelhouse.

"Bridge!"

I leaned over the voice-pipe.

"I think we're all right, sir. The course seems to fit, anyway."

The drizzle turned to mist in the early morning. My relief when *Juno* lightship loomed up was profound. We were in familiar waters again, and berthed at Spud Pier, Arromanches, on time. Our passengers had cars waiting for them and hurried ashore. Their luck was in—if only they knew it—and so was ours!

A week or so later at Milford Haven, with the ship in the hands of the yard, and the first lieutenant away on a navigation course, a signal was brought aboard in the middle of the night. I propped myself on my elbow and tore it open. My appointment had come through, but not to the 13th M.L. Flotilla as I had expected. Instead, I was to go to *M.L. 147* in command, and senior officer of the 20th M.L. Flotilla.

So it was Normandy again after all. I shook my head musingly and dropped off to sleep again.

CHAPTER VI

DUTCH INTERLUDE

I JOINED *M.L. 147* at Portsmouth, and was not impressed with my new command. Superficially smart—and she had carried the King on the occasion of his visit to the Normandy beaches —below decks she left much to be desired. Nor was she a happy ship. The coxswain had left under a cloud, and I was warned against other malcontents. There was an air of slackness and lack of discipline; I found requestmen to see me in private were being turned away. But there was no time then to sort things out, for we sailed almost immediately for the assault area.

S.S.E.F. welcomed me back with a broad grin when we went alongside his headquarters ship. "You've been a long time coming," he said. "What's happened to you?"

"Just arrived, sir, via Milford Haven," I replied. "You weren't really expecting me back, surely?"

But the Support Squadron commander only laughed again and slapped me on the shoulder.

Conditions had changed on the eastern flank since I went away. The weather was our worst enemy now. Night after night we were forced to abandon Trout Line to seek shelter with the L.C.G.s and L.C.F.s in Arromanches, and I took the opportunity to tighten up the ship's routine.

I was accustomed to a daily inspection of engine-room and fuel compartment bilges, and for all the other bilges to be dried out and cleaned weekly. The fuel compartment was supposedly pumped by hand, but I never saw a deck pump aboard. Eventually it transpired that the main bilge pump connection to the wardroom had been cut at the fuel compartment, which was not only against all regulations, but left the after part of the ship without means of pumping.

On my first rounds the engine-room reeked of petrol. The disregard of elementary fire precautions was appalling, and that at a time when more M.L.s had been lost through fire

than by enemy action. I was no engineer, but had seen an M.L. on fire, and that was impressive enough to imbue me with a healthy respect for high-octane petrol. For one thing, I insisted on the use of bilge extractor fans before starting engines, only to find that both fans were out of order—and had been ever since the motor mechanic had been aboard, so he averred.

The first lieutenant was a good chap, and we might have hit it off together in different circumstances, but his ways were not mine, and I was not sorry when he left for a command of his own in another flotilla. That same day we had a fire in the engine-room alongside the cruiser *Adventure*.

I was in the wheelhouse when the alarm was given, and dashed aft just as the motor mechanic shot out of the hatch with badly burned arms. There was a mass of flames below on the starboard side. I dropped the hatch and ordered the methyl bromide remote control lever to be pulled in the wheelhouse. It had no effect, and eventually we put out the blaze with Foamite extinguishers.

Apparently the motor mechanic was cleaning plugs in a bucket of paraffin—so he said—and was testing the spark when the bucket went up in flames. I suspected petrol, but let the matter drop when the motor mechanic went into hospital.

Trout Line patrol petered out quite suddenly. Havre fell; the battle ebbed away to the eastward, and we returned to Portsmouth for Channel escort work, but within a few weeks we found ourselves attached to Force T, with three other M.L.s of the Flotilla, working again as navigational leaders to landing craft and the Support Squadron.

A new first lieutenant joined from steam gunboats. He quickly sized up the situation and began to sort things out below decks. We had our technical equipment thoroughly overhauled, so that by the time we sailed from Southampton towards the end of October, 1944, I felt reasonably happy again.

Our departure for Ostend was not auspicious. We were due to sail at first light; some of the Force had anchored in the Solent off Gilkicker for the night; others lay in Southampton Water. But late that night Commander-in-Chief Portsmouth made a signal for all craft to proceed immediately, as fog was expected in the early morning. The task of assembling and

9 5th December, 1945. With Elizabeth and Dorothy at the Palace.

10 *Nancy Grey* at Pin Mill. Built by Shuttlewood at Paglesham just before the war after the style of a Thames barge, she makes a fine, roomy, shallow-draft yacht.

11   The Hard at Pin Mill, with the barge blocks on the right.

12a Goldsmith's *Cambria* carried away her sprit out by the Spitway and managed to limp back into Colne unaided.

b Elizabeth in sailing rig.

13*a* Becalmed under the trees.

b *P.A.M.* with grey-painted wale and gilt scrollwork, waiting to lock through at Allington.

14a Heaving up the gear. The anchor chain is cleared from the windlass barrel to make room for the stayfall.

b Horlock's *Repertor* coming up on our weather. She was built at Mistley in 1924.

15 *P.A.M.* running down Swin, with the Skipper by the lee rigging.
The foresail is sheeted permanently to the wooden horse.

16 *P.A.M.* beating up the Whitaker Channel.

sailing a large force of slow, cumbersome craft in the dark is no easy matter, yet somehow or other the main body got clear of Spithead soon after midnight.

We spent the night chasing up stragglers and checking up the port column. Signalling took too long; we had to sheer up alongside each craft in turn, hailing and getting a reply by megaphone that was more often than not inaudible above the noise of the engines.

" Watch yourself with these chaps," I remarked to my first lieutenant. " They'll prang you if you give 'em half a chance! "

We were nearly two hours working up the port column, and finally reported to the group commander just as navigation lights were seen to be converging on us from ahead. We had insufficient room to turn short round, and elected instead to pass ahead of the port column in order to run back and start checking the starboard column.

We rounded the leader rather closer than I cared, but the approaching ships were crossing our bows and left us little option but to keep wheel on, when suddenly I realized the second craft in the line was well out on the quarter of the leader and apparently steering his own course.

" Hard a-starboard," I shouted. " Full ahead together."

The engine-room responded quickly, and we surged ahead. " Midships."

The massive swim bows of an L.C.G. loomed up over our bridge. For a moment I thought we were clear, and I yelled " Hard a-port " in the hope of throwing our stern round.

It was too late. There was a great roar of water, then our radar tower crunched and crumbled. We heeled over till water surged aboard. For a few moments we were carried along broadside on. Then the way of the L.C.G. came off. We righted and came clear. Engine-room telegraphs were smashed; the helm was jammed hard over. One engine had stopped; the other was racing at full ahead. The midships Oerlikon had disappeared through the deck into the engine-room, but the stoker on duty had scrambled out. Now wreckage obstructed the hatches, but luckily the motor mechanic was a wiry man and managed to get below to switch off before we ran amok.

We mustered the hands. The midships Oerlikon gunner was missing; there was no sign of him beneath the wreckage of

his gun, and it seemed he must have gone overboard. We sounded all compartments and took stock of our damage. The engine-room and fuel compartments had borne the brunt of the collision. Topsides and upperworks were badly smashed, but I was glad to be able to signal the commander that we were in no immediate danger of sinking. The L.C.G. had sustained no damage; she came alongside before proceeding, and to our amazement the missing gunner stepped aboard. Apparently he had scrambled aboard the L.C.G. as her swim bows ground his gun through the deck.

Force T disappeared into the night, and I was left with an overwhelming sense of helplessness and futility. It all seemed unreal during the dark hours, but now in the first morning light the crumpled, canting radar tower and the sad mess of deck and topsides was only too apparent.

A corvette towed us back to Spithead. Later that day, berthed in front of the *Hornet* wardroom, I had the mortification of writing out an S.232—Report of Collision and Grounding.

Then *M.L. 902* came up overnight from Portland. I shipped aboard with my telegraphist and signalman, and sailed for Ostend, where Force T had assembled in the mine-blasted, desolated dock basins. A few nights later we set out for Walcheren.

Ours was the job of marking the route through the minefields. The night was uneventful, dark and quiet. M.L.s anchored in predetermined positions and hung out dimmed blue lights. Then we turned in towards West Kapelle. Morning came, with hardly a ripple on the water; sand dunes and tower and houses stood out with incredible clarity.

The first of the assault craft began to turn in as we prepared to take up our own position about five miles off shore. We dropped anchor. Almost immediately came flashes from West Kapelle, followed by the whine of shells. The Domburg batteries opened up too, and we lay there like a sitting duck, for we could do nothing but watch for the flashes and keep our fingers crossed. We were straddled time and again until orders came to withdraw.

It was then I got hit. A near miss off the port bow peppered us with shell fragments, and I found myself lying on deck looking at my toes, unable to move. There was no pain; I remember

58

no sensation at all—just complete paralysis. At last, to my unutterable joy, after what seemed an eternity, I found I could wriggle my toes . . . and fingers . . . then life came surging back. I scrambled up. Only my neck felt dead.

By this time the shore batteries had our range. It could only be a matter of minutes before we were hit. Weighing by hand was too slow, and we decided to slip. As we went astern and the cable ran out, I thought of Cul Bay.

"How's it fastened to the clench, Number One?"

"With a lashing, sir, I think."

We never saw the end go. Had there been a shackle, it would still have gone.

The story of the assault on Walcheren is well known; how the Support Squadron engaged the batteries, drew their fire, and was cut to pieces; how the attack was pressed home and the Commandos landed; how the Scheldt was swept and the port of Antwerp opened to Allied shipping. All this is history, but I saw little of it, for I took passage back to Ostend aboard *M.L. 146*, whose bridge had been smashed and Chris Cookson, the commanding officer, killed with three of his crew in a gallant attempt to mark the shoals off West Kapelle. I woke in hospital at Ostend to find a grizzled old bearded veteran in the opposite bed. We needed no introduction, for it was his L.C.G. that had so forcibly boarded us off Selsea Bill!

After a few days at Ostend, and three weeks at Haslar, where an abortive attempt was made to get the fragment of shell out of my neck, I went back to the Flotilla in command of *M.L. 146*, now just completing refit at Portland. She was a first-class ship in every way. The coxswain was highly efficient; so, too, was the hefty young first lieutenant, who had distinguished himself at Walcheren, and who still retained an inordinate schoolboy appetite for jam tarts. The messdeck was crowded, but the spirit among the crew was magnificent. *M.L. 146* was a happy ship.

During the early months of 1945 we worked out of Portland on Channel escort duties, rolling our decks under in the winter gales, chasing through fog with the aid of radar and Q.H., revelling in the spring sunshine, with St. Catherine's and the white cliffs of St. Albans as our landfalls.

Then, in April, we sailed for Holland to work in the East Scheldt. Our base was Wemeldinge, on the South Beveland Canal, a typical Dutch village boasting a couple of windmills, and where all but the youngest of the women still wore traditional costume. They were good to our ship's company; the family men joined in the home life, and the younger lads found dancing partners at nearby Yeserke, the centre of the Dutch oyster culture.

The tide of battle had passed by after the Canadians overran this part of Holland some months before. The lock gates were in use again, and it was difficult to realize at times that the Germans were still in possession of Tholen and Schouen across on the other side of the East Scheldt. Ours was a night patrol, sailing at dusk to a position in the middle of the estuary to maintain a radar watch throughout the dark hours. Two L.C.S.(M.)s—landing craft support (medium)—armed with 0.5 machine guns, were attached to deal with any small enemy craft that might venture out. It had been an interesting job, but the war in Europe was drawing to a close, and the last few nights had been quiet and uneventful.

Then, one night . . .

"Captain, sir. From the first lieutenant. Permission to test guns, sir, please?"

The coxswain's cheerful face withdrew from the wardroom doorway. A few moments later the midships Oerlikon opened up with a short burst, followed by the twin guns overhead.

Presently the first lieutenant came clattering down.

"All set, Number One?"

"Gear tested and correct, sir. The L.C.S.(M.)s left harbour ten minutes ago."

"What sort of a night?"

"Not too bad. It's going to be mighty dark, though. I told Cox'n harbour stations in ten minutes if that's all right with you."

On deck all was peaceful except for the clanking of the boom across the entrance of the small harbour. Most of the crew, with lifebelts on, were leaning over the guard rails chatting with our sister ship. It was her night in. On the dyke the good folk of Wemeldinge were taking the air.

The first lieutenant joined me. It was time to get away, for

60

the light was failing fast. We made our way to the bridge where the signalman was chalking up the recognition signals for the night.

Coxswain was waiting by the messdeck hatch.

" Harbour stations, sir? "

" Yes, please."

The rest of the crew came tumbling up.

" Stand by your lines! "

The engines burst into life, and settled to a dull roar.

" All ready, sir."

" Single up to your backspring, Number One. Starb'd thirty, Cox'n."

Our stern was swinging out with the creep of the propellers. I rang down slow astern on the starboard engine and motioned for the backspring to be cast off. " Midships, Cox'n."

" Wheel's amidships, sir! "

" All gone, sir," sang out the first lieutenant. " Hands fall in for'ard! "

Slowly we backed out from our berth and swung round the wrecked German flak ship in the middle of the little harbour, then corkscrewed our way through the gate in the boom. Dutch soldiers were already standing by with their under-water bombs, which they pitched into the entrance every twenty minutes throughout the night as a deterrent to any frogman that might be venturing in for another crack at the lock gates.

The hands fell out, and doubled away to secure for sea. Half ahead now, and we rolled a little in the short seas. Over on the other side of the Scheldt the low silhouette of Tholen and Schouen still showed up in the gathering gloom, with the tower at Zierikzee prominent away to the northward.

The navigating officer was singing out the new course from the wheelhouse.

" Thank you. Port twenty, Cox'n; . . . ease to ten. Steady on north thirty-eight west."

The first lieutenant stood by the standard compass in the middle of the bridge. " Sing out when you're on, Cox'n."

" On now, sir."

" Steer forty."

" Steady on north forty west, sir."

61

Presently the forward lookout hailed the bridge. " Object bearing red two-O! "

I picked up my glasses.

" Plot! "

" Plot—bridge," answered the navigator.

" Small buoy bearing fine on the port bow."

" That's right. Leave it to port. You're all clear then up to Surrey."

Surrey was the code name for a red-flashing buoy off the entrance to the Zandcreek separating North and South Beveland. It was one of three buoys laid by a Trinity House vessel in the East Scheldt. The Germans shelled her at the time, and later blew up the eastern buoy off Collijnsplaat. The middle buoy remained, and was known to us as Blockshop, but the light was dim and unreliable.

It was quite dark now and overcast.

" Plot! Surrey's coming abeam."

" Course from Surrey, sir, north sixty-four west."

" Starb'd twenty, Cox'n."

This was the worst part, driving across the stream towards the shallows where the small can marking the temporary mooring was too inconspicuous for our radar to pick up with certainty. There was rain in the wind, too.

" How's the water, Plot? "

" Echo-sounder gives seventeen feet, shoaling gradually. Two more minutes to run."

" Radar! "

" Radar—bridge! "

" Anything right ahead? "

" The banks are just uncovering, sir. . . . Here we are, sir. Echo right ahead, range four hundred."

" Plot—bridge! One minute to run."

Soon there came a hail from the foredeck. " Object fine on the port bow."

One of the L.C.S.(M.)s had already picked up the mooring buoy. We ranged slowly alongside, and they passed it across on a heaving line.

" All fast! "

" Ring off, Cox'n."

62

The two L.C.S. (M.)s secured on our starboard side and the marine officers in command came up on the bridge.

"Pot of coffee on the hatch, sir."

"Thanks, Cox'n."

We arranged the routine patrols for the night. The outboard craft was to slip at midnight for a trip past Blockshop to Collijnsplaat, and the other was to make a similar run at two o'clock. That would see us through the darkest hours, for the moon would be up in the early morning.

We settled to the usual night watches. The navigator turned in, but the first lieutenant stood propped in the opposite corner of the bridge, with hands in pocket and coat collar turned up. The bridge lookout hung over the dodger; the signalman leaned against the messdeck hatch, with the R/T set crackling quietly by his side. Overhead, the radar aerial whined round and round in the perspex dome. Snatches of conversation came up the W/T office voice-pipe from time to time, but there was hardly a word spoken on deck. Gun crews and lookouts might well have been asleep, yet when a flare went up away to the north-east, there came an immediate chorus; "Flare, green four-five!"

The first lieutenant huddled round the standard compass for a bearing, then swung himself below into the wheelhouse.

"Bridge! that flare must be away over the seaward tip of Schouen."

"Thank you, Number One."

For a brief spell the lookouts stamped and stretched, then the ship settled again to silence. Suddenly the bell rang from the radar office.

"Captain, sir. There's an echo bearing red six-five, range fourteen hundred. It's a bit jumpy, though, and I wouldn't be too sure of it."

There was nothing to be seen to port except the flashing Surrey buoy, but the first lieutenant came to life again, and dropped below. I could hear him talking with the radar operator, then he called the bridge.

"Course seems rather erratic, but it seems to be making vaguely for Zandcreek. . . . It's stopped now. Shouldn't think it's anything to worry about."

It could be a flight of birds, maybe, or tide rip, or just a

63

spot of fluorescent cussedness on the screen—gremlins we usually called them.

"What's the time, Number One? "

"A quarter to twelve."

"Signalman, my compliments to the commanding officer of the outboard L.C.S.(M.), and ask him to step up to the bridge."

Within a few moments a short, stocky figure came chasing aboard.

"Sorry to haul you out before your time," I said, "but there's a gremlin playing around in the entrance to Zandcreek. I thought you might care to take a look round."

"Right you are. We'll get cracking."

As he went, the other commanding officer came bustling up. "What's this going on, sir? You won't leave us out of the party, surely?"

"But it's only a gremlin; besides, you've got a patrol at two o'clock."

"Come on, sir. Be a sport. Two of us are better than one, you know."

I had not the heart to refuse. "All right. You'll have to hurry, though."

The first craft was already casting off.

"What's their course, Number One? "

"Due west, sir."

Within a few moments the second craft was away, swallowed up in the darkness. We were hardly likely to pick them up on our P.P.I. until they were 300 yards off, when the two small craft in company would probably appear as a single object —just a pinpoint of fluorescence creeping over towards the land.

"Let me know when you pick them up, Radar."

"Haven't got them yet, sir. There's a lot of grass and interference just now."

The senior radar operator came up from below and slipped into the wheelhouse. Soon ranges and bearings were being passed in rapid succession to the first lieutenant, who was at work on the chart keeping the plot.

"Echo seems to be making for the land. Suggest they alter course twenty degrees to starboard."

"Signalman, make by R/T—steer twenty degrees to starboard."

"Aye, aye, sir. This is Lodestone. Sneeze two. I say again, sneeze two . . . Message passed, sir."

The radar P.P.I. was clearer now; it seemed, after all, that the gremlin had taken on a more definite form and was holding a steady course, with the L.C.S.(M.)s in company two cables astern. But the first lieutenant was getting perturbed about the water.

"They're getting pretty close inshore, sir."

"Yes, and it's mighty dark still. What's the bottom like?"

"It should be mud, but I wouldn't be sure just off the point there."

"Signalman, tell 'em to watch out for the putty."

"Plot—bridge! Echo's bearing away to starboard. Suggest L.C.S.(M.)s alter course eighty degrees to starboard."

"Sneeze eight, Signalman. . . . How are they doing, Number One?"

"They seem to be opening slightly now, sir." The minutes passed. "Soon be coming up to Blockshop."

"Radar—bridge! Passing out of range, sir."

Another five minutes, and still no report from the L.C.S.(M.)s.

"Signalman, ask them to indicate their position."

"Indicate position. Aye, aye, sir."

Back came the replies: "Approaching Collijnsplaat."

"Very good. Tell them to return."

"Hullo, Clover. Hullo, Violet. This is Lodestone. Snuffle. I say again, snuffle. . . . Message passed, sir."

"Well, what d'you make of it all? " I asked.

A long pause, then: "I don't know. It looked for all the world like a gremlin to start with, but it was a good sharp echo afterwards."

We lapsed into silence. Of course, it *might* have been an explosive motor-boat; one had been captured in these waters only a few weeks before. Ought we to have slipped and got under way ourselves? Doubts always start creeping in after the event. If only our chaps had sighted something we should have had more to work on.

"Object red two-five!"

The first lieutenant called for a couple of hands and berthed

65

the L.C.S.(M.) alongside. The commanding officer came up
to the bridge very pugnacious and full of indignation.

"God! What a pity! I thought you were letting us go
across and beat 'em up on the other side."

I grinned. "Sorry, but you got out of range. Did you see
anything at all? "

"Not a blind thing."

"Where's your pal? "

"Not the faintest idea."

"But surely you've been in company all the time, haven't
you? "

"No, we never saw him from the time we slipped."

A prickly heat crept up my spine. God! What sort of target
was this? Had we been vectoring one L.C.S.(M.) on the other?
Anyway, it was no place for two small craft to be milling
around on their own, for these Marines were keen, light-
triggered types.

There was nothing to be done about it. I sent him to look
at the plot. Soon the other L.C.S.(M.) hove in sight and secured
alongside.

"Never saw a thing, sir. Awful shame! My chaps were just
itching for a scrap."

"I bet they were," I replied grimly. "You must have been
very close to the land at one time."

"Yes, we had just swung off to starboard when you came
up on the R/T. What was it, d'you think? "

"Oh, just a gremlin." It had been to start with, anyway!

Presently, when the Marines had returned aboard their own
craft, the first lieutenant came up on the bridge again and
hunched himself in the corner, with his chin tucked in his polo-
necked sweater.

"I've a horrid suspicion, Number One——"

"Yes, sir. I know."

"We'll take care they keep in company next time."

"I never dreamed they weren't together."

"Nor me, for that matter. . . . Thanks be to heaven they're
back! "

After a while hot soup and toast appeared on the bridge,
and the navigator came up to stand his watch.

"Everything quiet? " he asked.

"Pretty quiet. We had the L.C.S.(M.)s out chasing gremlins a little while back."

"Any joy, sir?"

"Never saw a thing, did they, Number One?"

* * * * *

We were in Wemeldinge the night the Germans threw up the sponge in Holland. As if by magic, flags flew from every house. Within an hour the town band assembled, their instruments green with verdigris, and the staid, sober folk gave themselves up to a night of dancing, singing and cheering round the village. Next morning we all looked somewhat sheepish and ashamed of ourselves.

We were in Antwerp for V.E. Day, but the celebrations seemed less spontaneous and we were rather concerned with the safety of our ship from rockets and flares. Nevertheless, the first lieutenant joined me next day in an ice-cream crawl through the city. We had never seen such magnificent confections. Only when we repaired aboard, replete and well satisfied, did we find port orders waiting for us, with strict instructions that ices were suspect in Antwerp and not to be eaten by naval personnel under dire penalties. But we had no regrets!

Our patrol finished, we had the job of escorting the small landing craft of Force T that had taken part in the Rhine crossings back to Ostend for shipment to England. We were two weeks on the job, and the day before we were to sail for Southampton the crew gave a party for their Dutch friends. The messdeck was decorated with bunting, and the guests arrived in their Sunday best for a gargantuan feast. It was the children's day, though. They came in party clothes, the most delightful children imaginable, and once their shyness had worn off, they tucked in as only children can. It was a tired and happy crowd that went ashore that night.

Next morning, as we cast off for the last time, there were kiddies crying on the quayside. I fancy there were several moist eyes among the crew. In fact, I know there were!

Back in Southampton, with a barrel of oysters as a souvenir from Yeserke, we bade farewell to the Naval Commander Force T and the Commander of the Support Squadron. The oysters were consumed. Force T was disbanded.

After a short refit in Portland, we sailed for Cuxhaven, where

67

the remainder of the Flotilla were patrolling and showing the flag. But at Ramsgate we had orders from the Admiralty to put into port pending further instructions. Coastal forces were being reduced. There were rumours of paying off, and we had visions of appointments in the Far East. Meantime, we lay in Ramsgate Inner Harbour and gave leave to the ship's company.

Then, one evening, I caught sight of a Thames barge— Everard's *Lady Mary*—standing in, and I went to the pierhead to watch her as she picked up her mainsail and came surging in with a fine quartering breeze. There were only two aboard, the skipper at the wheel and the young mate struggling with the lower brails.

As she came past, the skipper sang out: "Let go fores'l when you like . . . and tops'l."

Lady Mary luffed up for the mooring buoy in the middle of the harbour. Slowly her way came off until she lay a yard or so off, and I expected to see the mate tumble into the boat and make fast. But no, the skipper ran forward and touched down the anchor, then went off in the boat himself with a line.

Next morning, when they were loading coke in the Inner Harbour, I went round for a chat with the skipper.

"I saw you come in yesterday," I said. "Nice to see a barge under sail again."

The skipper smiled a slow, gentle smile, as if he guessed my thoughts. "We didn't quite fetch the buoy," he replied, then nodded towards the mate, busy trimming cargo in the hold. "He's not much of a hand in a boat yet. Can't expect everything at once, though. Up to the end of last week he was still serving groceries over the counter up at Woolwich."

I rejoiced to find how my pulse quickened. The war was over as far as I was concerned. Coastal Forces and Combined Operations were fading, and barges were looming up again.

CHAPTER VII

SWALLOWING THE ANCHOR

" It doesn't look too good, does it? "

I was on leave pending appointment, having paid off *M.L. 146,* and here we were, Dorothy and I, standing in *June's* saloon feeling thoroughly despondent.

The decks were leaking badly, and there were large rusty stains where water had seeped through on the settees. Drips of moisture hung in clusters from the cabin top. The flooring had given way beneath the fireplace, and the stove was rusty and falling to pieces. Of course, she *could* be done up, but with all the time and money spent on her, she would still be a very old barge at the end of it. Then there was the difficulty of getting work done, and the scarcity of materials, too. Better to make a clean break. I hated patching, anyway.

We left *June* in Conyer Creek and returned to Tankerton, where Dorothy had been living in a furnished bungalow for the last year of the war. Our furniture was stowed in an owl-frequented loft of the old Conyer cement works in company with *June's* sails and gear. The chance of getting another barge seemed very remote; many had been taken up by the Government, while those still trading were earning good money. Besides, we had Elizabeth now, and a little girl would likely prove too much of a responsibility, so Dorothy thought.

" We'd better look for a house," she said.

" Are you sure you know what you want? " I asked, for even in the old days we had rebelled at the idea of settling down to suburban life.

" I think so," she replied, somewhat dubiously. " Something small and unusual—on its own, of course, yet not too far from shops and places. It'll have to be near the sea somewhere, or on some creek or other. And I suppose you'll want to get to London? "

" I'm afraid so," though I was far from enamoured at the prospect.

69

"Well, that means we'd have to be near a station. Would Whitstable be too far? "

" I shouldn't think so." True, it was about sixty miles out, but when we brought *June* into Whitstable before the war, I had found the journey reasonable enough.

Dorothy was already struggling into a coat. "Come on, then. Let's have a look at old Whitstable and see what's going."

Many of the houses along the sea wall were barricaded and empty, and the beach was fringed with concrete pillars and a network of steel defences festooned with barbed wire. But the foreshore was not entirely deserted, for the shipyards were busy with wooden motor fishing vessels for the Navy. There were yachts beached above high-water level, and oyster smacks; the sailing barge *Savoy*, too, was on the ways, with her bows towering high above the cluster of sheds.

Close by the horse bridge, where carts came over the sea wall not so very long back after coal and timber and ballast from sailing barges lying on the foreshore, the sea wall narrowed, with houses on either side. There were cottages to landward, and larger, detached houses backing on the beach. The first three were occupied, but the house at the end, flanking the short promenade, was empty and for sale. It was a three-gabled house, with one part of yellow weatherboard, and the other of red brick.

"This looks rather nice," Dorothy exclaimed, and dived down a small side turning to the beach. "Come and have a look."

The beach itself was still cluttered up with fortifications, and quite impassable, but it was easy to imagine how nice the place could be in peacetime, in spite of the broken, boarded windows.

" Is it worth inquiring about? " I asked, but Dorothy shook her head.

" It's far too large. I'd never be able to run a house that size."

It was surprisingly mild just here, for the curve of the land and the harbour jetty served to shelter us from the cold north-easterly. This was by far the most pleasant part of Whitstable, with its quaint houses and fishermen's sheds. There was a blacksmith, too, and sailmaker's loft and shipchandler's store.

And in the harbour were sailing barges. We stood for a while watching an old man with flowing white whiskers opening sacks at the top of a polished wooden shute to send golden Kentish wheat cascading into the open hold of the *Violet*, while the young barge skipper, who remembered us from pre-war days, trimmed the wheat and still found time to joke with the ancient on the quay.

But it was on the way home we came across a dream house set in the wooden slopes beneath Tankerton Castle. It was a yellow-painted, shingle-boarded house right on the sea front, empty and dilapidated. Many of the windows were broken, and tiles had fallen from the roof. The garden, too, was overgrown. The house itself was not large, and seemed to be built around a central room, with a loggia on the style of an American colonial house. We tried to get into the garden, but the gates in the tall wooden fence were padlocked.

"I wonder if it *is* for sale," Dorothy asked, after she had peered through the fence for some time. "I don't see any house agents' names up anywhere. The owners might be glad to sell, though. It's worth trying to find out."

We tried the rating office, but the little man seemed rather loth to give us the owner's name and address, and referred us to a firm of house agents.

Here the reception was more cordial, for business was beginning to look up, and there was an atmosphere of warmth and cheerfulness.

"Do please sit down. Take this seat by the fire, madam." Then, standing back, and beaming at us both: "Now, what can I do for you?"

"Well, you see . . ." we both began, so I grinned at Dorothy and left her to go on with the story.

She told him about the house under the cliff. Did he know the owner, and was it for sale?

The beaming smile seemed to me to be rather less expansive. "Why, yes, we know all about *that* place."

"That's fine. The man in the rates office told us you'd probably be able to help. Perhaps you'd let us have the key so that we can see over the house."

"I'm sorry, madam, but—er—the fact is, we haven't the key just now."

The smile was definitely on the wane. It became confiding and almost mystical, so that Dorothy and I found ourselves leaning forward instinctively to hang on the hushed words that were surely coming. Nor were we disappointed.

"You see, the—er—owner just couldn't make up his mind. At first he wanted £1,500, and we put the house on our books. Then, of course, property started appreciating in value, and no sooner had we placed inquiries before him than he jumped his price. Started talking of £2,500. In the end we sent the key back to him. Really, I mean, you can't do business like that! Most unsatisfactory! "

It was obvious to us that the owner had no intention of selling. Why should he?

"Perhaps he hopes to come back to the house himself," I suggested.

"But, my dear sir, we had it on our books, so he must have wanted to sell! "

Obviously, there was nothing more to be said on the subject. After a suitable pause, he opened a black-covered book and rapidly ran his fingers down the page.

"Ah! " A smile crept across his face again. "Now, here's a house that should meet your requirements. A lovely modern place, quite in the country, with six bedrooms, two bathrooms, three reception rooms, large garden. How does that sound, sir? "

"Awful! " I muttered. "You see, that's exactly what we don't want."

"But, my dear sir, it's a magnificent place! "

"Yes, yes, I know. It's every bit as good as you say, no doubt, but we don't want a big modern place in the country. It's an old house with character we're after—something out of the ordinary."

"Six bedrooms, indeed! " echoed Dorothy. "Whoever's going to look after a place like that, I ask you? "

"Oh, I forgot to mention, there are servants' quarters, too."

"Fat lot of good they'd be! "

"And who wants a large garden? " I added quickly. "I'd have to be working all the time and never get any sailing. Besides, we're after a place by the sea. What else did you say? Two garages. Why, I haven't even one car, let alone two! "

But our friend, the house agent, was insistent upon playing the game through to the bitter end. He stood in front of the fire, with feet apart and thumbs stuck in his waistcoat.

"It's cheap at the price. Dirt cheap, in fact. It's only £4,000."

Dorothy and I looked at each other and burst into laughter.

"I'm sorry," I said at last. "You've got the wrong idea entirely. I'm not a millionaire, and we don't want a big house. We don't even want a small house—at least, not the ordinary sort. And I don't know that we want a garden particularly, so long as it's by the sea."

"It'll have to be near a station for the London trains."

"And near the shops," I added.

"And away from busy roads because of Elizabeth."

"And—oh, lots of things, but I don't suppose you'd ever have such a place on your books for the simple reason people never sell the sort of house we're after."

I reached for my cap and we rose to go. The house agent was very charming still, and promised to let us know as soon as he had anything suitable, but I could see his heart was no longer with us. He was accustomed to deal in bricks and mortar and hard cash; whimsical fancies were not part of his stock-in-trade. Besides, there were plenty of other people waiting, with more normal requirements.

It was obvious that sooner or later our landlady would want her bungalow again, either for herself or for summer letting. We could not complain; the understanding was quite clear that we should have it until the end of the war in Europe. Besides, it was furnished, and, naturally, we wanted to have our own furniture out of store.

Dorothy tried the house agents again, but everybody seemed to be after houses and prices were soaring. We visited *June* again, with the idea, possibly, of buying another barge and having the gear transferred. But sailing barges were scarce, for there had been considerable wastage during the war. *Alderman* and *Knowles* were lost on the Clyde; *Tam o' Shanter*, wheat-laden, was lost in the Spitway through stress of weather, and *Castanet* hit a wreck in the Wallet; *Bijou* was blitzed alongside the quay at Mistley, *Excelsior* at Ipswich, *R. S. Jackson* in London, *Enchantress* in the Royal Albert Docks . . .

Lady Roseberry and *Doris* were mined off Dunkirk, while

73

Barbara Jean, Duchess, Lark, Aidie, Royalty and *Ethel Everard* were lost on the beaches.

Emma was mined at Rotherhithe, and many others in the Thames Estuary; *H.K.D.* by the Outer Bar Buoy, *Globe* just outside Sheerness Harbour, *Rosmé* by the S.E. Maplin, *Bankside* and *J.B.W.* in S.W. Reach, *Ailsa* by the Whitaker, *Blue Mermaid* and *Resolute* in the Wallet, *Gertrude May* out by the Gunfleet . . .

A great number had been engaged on powder work and mine-watching in the Thames and Medway, and those coming off service were sadly lacking in gear. What was worse, many of the barges were reputed to be riddled with worm.

"Lor' love us, gov'nor," exclaimed the skipper of *The Brownie*, "one of our'n come up on the yard the other day —*Queen*, it was—and I see them take a worm out of her that long," and he held his arms apart like a fisherman. "As big round as my thumb. Fair turned me up!"

His opinion was backed up by the manager of a firm with a number of barges for sale. He warned me to have nothing to do with them. Even had they been sound, the prices ranging up to £650 would have resulted in an expensive yacht barge. It was a far call from the day we bought *June* complete with gear and boat for £50, but that was in 1933, when trade was bad and barges were a drug on the market.

In desperation we fitted out *June's* boat in the barge shed at Conyer. We should at least have something to sail!

Whitstable was a great attraction; the local brigs and schooners and ketches had gone, but barges were trading there still. We watched *Azima* coming in, her red sails standing out vividly against the clear blue of the summer sky. The mainsail was already furled; as she came in past the end of the jetty down dropped the foresail . . . then topsail headstick. Still she carried her way, gliding up the harbour. The mate hove a line to us on the knuckle of the quay and I made it fast. Deftly he took a turn and the barge brought up to berth alongside the elevator.

It was all so workaday and commonplace, yet to us so reminiscent of pre-war days. This was where we belonged, down here by the harbour.

We strolled on past the tarred and weather-boarded fisher-

men's sheds to the sea wall, where the good folk of Whitstable gathered in the quiet of the summer evening to sit and gossip while the sun went down in a blaze of glory behind the Isle of Sheppey, across the bay.

The big house we had noticed before stood at the end of the short promenade.

"I wonder if it's still empty," Dorothy remarked. "What a view there must be from those beach windows! Just look at that sunset!"

We strolled on.

"Good heavens!" Dorothy stopped short and grabbed my arm. "Look! There are people living in the wooden part."

"So they are. Curtains up, too. Somebody's lucky."

But Dorothy was still excited.

"Don't you see, the wooden part has got folk in, but the brick part is empty. Look, there's the 'For Sale' notice still up in the window."

"I do believe you're right," I exclaimed, and stood on the step to peer between the slats of the boarded window. "Why, this part is a separate house altogether."

"I can't imagine why we ever thought it was one," said Dorothy, as she peered up at the stone lintel. "It's even got its own name. I can just make it out. It's called 'The Nore.'"

We went round to the side of the house. Most of the beach fortifications had gone. The gate in the brick wall that led down to the beach was bolted, but we peered through the grille. Somebody had been at work on the house, for there were new tiles underneath each of the enormous bay windows. Our curiosity got the better of us, and we clambered round the partially demolished side wall. The house was obviously built round the view; the windows overlooking the anchorage and the entire Thames Estuary so fired our imagination that it was easy to ignore the broken panes and weathered paintwork.

There were four stories on the seaward side. The semi-basement opened on to the beach, with a few steps down from the side gate. This room was full of builder's gear and rubbish, for somebody had been putting in a new ceiling and concrete floors. Above this, on the level of the sea wall, came the ground floor, with a door opening on to a small, tumble-down wooden balcony, with steps down to the beach.

All this time we had hardly said a word.

" Well," I said at last, "what d'you make of it? "

" It's just the very place we've been looking for."

I nodded. The surprising thing was that it was still empty. Perhaps the foundations were wrong, or the drains, or roof. I knew nothing about houses, yet this one conveyed an impression of solidity.

Dorothy was full of excitement. She inquired at the neighbouring house about "The Nore," but they had only moved in recently and could not tell us much. Were we thinking of taking it? There was some talk of it being let, though they could not say for certain. Apparently there had been an old chap working on the house. Had we tried knocking?

There was no response to our hearty bang that reverberated through the empty house, and we went round to the beach and clambered up on the rickety balcony.

" He *is* there," Dorothy whispered, and rapped on the window.

Somebody was putting on his coat. I do not think he heard our knock, but happened to catch sight of us as he turned round. The door was unbolted, and a wizened old man with a stoop and white drooping moustache peered at us over the top of his glasses.

" I reckon that must have been you knocking at the front door just now," he said. " I half thought I heard somebody."

" We're awfully sorry to worry you if you're just going," Dorothy began, " but we're so keen on the house that we wondered if we could have a quick look over it."

" Well, I was just getting off home to me supper, but you can have a look round if you like. Haven't been able to get the place straight yet."

" Has it been empty long? " I asked.

" Eh? You'll have to speak up. I'm a bit deaf. How long? I don't know for sure, but there's been nobody here since I come down to Whitstable time o' the London blitz."

It was getting late. The sun was dropping behind Sheppey, and the whole of the western sky was a blaze of red and gold. Dorothy and I stood entranced in the partially boarded bay window. The paper hung in strips from the cracked and broken walls; the electric light fittings were smashed, and the paint-

76

work dirty and worn; all this was forgotten in the magnificence of the view.

"It's better upstairs," said the old chap quietly. "Had to board everything up down here to keep the kids out."

We walked through into the hall, where the twisted remains of a stained-glass window lay on the floor. There were stairs tucked away behind doors leading down to the basement, and a twisting staircase to the upper floors, the whole rather cunningly contrived with an attractive grille effect.

There was another small room at the front of the house, opening off the hall. It was quite bare.

"I should have thought this would have been the kitchen," Dorothy remarked, with what I already perceived to be something of a proprietary air.

"Don't go building too many castles," I whispered.

"The kitchen's downstairs," said the old chap. "Not that there's much to show for it."

"Oh!" Dorothy tossed her head. "I'd jolly soon change that. This is where the kitchen should be."

I led her into the hall. "We'd better hurry. We're keeping this gentleman from his supper."

"That's all right. Don't you worry yourselves about me. There's only meself to look after at home, and my little bit o' watercress won't get cold."

He shuffled off down below while Dorothy and I went upstairs. Quite a number of the banister rails were missing; I remembered seeing the remains of one of them in the small room grate. Upstairs, conditions were not too bad. There were two bedrooms and a bathroom, but it was the big built-in ship's bunk in the small bedroom that caught our eye, a massive affair, nine feet long and nearly five feet high, with drawers beneath, and a wardrobe at either end. The room was quite presentable, in spite of a smashed window frame and the electricity meter jammed up the chimney.

The bathroom was more depressing, for the wash basin had gone completely, and the gas geyser was falling to pieces. The bath, too, was somewhat the worse for wear, as if somebody with hobnailed boots had forgotten to undress.

But any doubts we may have entertained were again set at

rest as soon as we entered the big bedroom with the bay window overlooking the beach.

"Gosh! What a view!"

The sun was nearly gone, and everything was suffused in a pink ethereal glow.

"This is the house for us," Dorothy declared. "I've never seen anything like it before."

"True enough," I replied. "I'm all for it, too, but it will be almost as bad as doing up *June,* and heaven only knows the cost. We'd better take a quick look upstairs and let the old chap go home."

The top floor comprised just one large garret room, with two fanlights at one end, and a couple of barricaded and broken glass sliding doors leading to a balcony. There had been two rooms at one time, but the partition had largely disappeared, and the clutter of dust and wallpaper and general filth was indescribable.

"Seen enough?"

Dorothy nodded. "This dirt doesn't worry me. I'd soon get this lot cleaned up."

Downstairs in the hall the old chap was waiting for us.

"So sorry to have kept you," Dorothy said.

"That's all right. What did you think of it?"

"Lovely! At least, it will be when it's done up."

"That's the trouble of it. There's a rare lot wants doing. I've been working on the place for nigh on three months and got precious little to show for it. The old doctor, he comes down and has a look round and says, 'You might just do it up, Mellor, and give it a splash of colour.' He don't realize how much there's to do. What with the floors and ceilings downstairs, and the new boards up here, and the tiles outside, and the gutter drain pipes all blocked up and windows smashed. You never get to the end of it."

"What's happening to the house, then?"

"Well, the doctor's talking of letting as soon as it's done up. Artist and her husband, so I heard. 'Don't you worry about doing much, Mellor,' says the doctor. 'Just colour the walls and let 'em get in.' That's all very well, but what with shortage of stuff and one thing and another, it's the devil of a job, I can tell you."

"I suppose it is difficult just now," I murmured.

"I should say it is. Why, it's worse now than what it was during the war. And when I tell the doctor I can't do this and that, he just laughs and says worse things happen at sea."

The blue eyes were twinkling over his spectacles. "And so it goes on."

"Do you think the owner would sell?" I asked.

"Well, he did talk of £950 at one time, but I don't think he's really keen on selling. He don't come down much now, but this used to be a sort of convalescent home of his, and he set a lot of store by it. He's a wonderful old man—vegetarian and a great one for sunshine. The artist lady who's supposed to be having the house did say they'd be willing to give up meat, too. What's more, they'd let the doctor have his bunk room whenever he wanted to come down. Why don't you make him an offer for the place when it's done up, that's what I'd do, and see what he says. Well, if you like to come down, I'll let you out through the beach door."

The larder and coal store were at the foot of the stairs, and two rooms. One had a sink installed and was obviously the scullery, but the windows were small and set high in the wall; the other was the kitchen, with rusted remains of a Dutch over. There were possibilities in this room, as the windows and door opened on to the beach although some three feet down.

"You'd better take this card," said the old chap, after he had carefully padlocked the door behind us. "I've got one here somewhere in my pocket-book. You'll know where to find me then. Good-night."

I took the card and read the name aloud: "*Henry Beevers Mellor, Stone Mason and Builder.*" The West Ham address was neatly ruled out, and "*Albion House, Harbour Place, Whitstable,*" inserted in a fine scholarly hand.

That night Dorothy and I lay awake for several hours talking things over. One thing was certain: we were both smitten with "The Nore." How much the repairs would cost, neither of us had the least idea, but if we could manage to buy the house for about £700 as it stood, we could afford to have it done up to our own ideas.

In the end I wrote a short letter asking if "The Nore" was

for sale, and if so, whether the owner was open for an offer. Back came the reply written in a spidery hand:—

" Preston.
" 6.8.45.

" Dear Sir,
" The price for 'The Nore' as it stands, with right to rebuild a hut on the shore front for boat mooring, etc., is £985. I am not open to an offer, and once it is completely refitted I shall return to it and shall not sell it at any price. It is too delightful a little treasure to lose.
" (Sgd.) JOSIAH OLDFIELD,
" Lt.-Colonel, R.A.M.C."

Dorothy's face fell. " Well," she said despondently, " we can't force him to sell if he wants to come and live there, can we? "

I read it through again. " Well, I don't know. It doesn't seem too bad."

" But he says he won't sell at any price."

" I read it to mean he'll sell as it stands for £985, but once it's done up he'll hang on to it. The question is, can we run to his price? "

" For heaven's sake pay what he asks," Dorothy exclaimed, brightening visibly. " I expect old Mr. Mellor would stay on and see the job through for us. He'd probably be less expensive than regular builders."

" Maybe he would," I replied, with a laugh, " but goodness knows when we'd get possession at the rate he's going."

We went down to " The Nore " again, and immediately fell under its spell. Elizabeth came with us; she clattered all over the house, played hide-and-seek in the wardrobes of the bunk, which she claimed for her own, then demanded her bathing costume. It was low tide, and the flats were uncovered, so we let her go, and she was soon splashing about in the shallow pools.

Meantime we tackled Mr. Mellor. Could he please give us the benefit of his experience and say candidly what he thought of the house?

He blinked at us over the top of his spectacles. " The house is all right—about forty years old, I should say. It's been good

in its time. I mean, look at that fireplace with the Dutch tiles and that wooden overmantel. It ain't exactly modern style, I know, but it's been put in by somebody as knows what he's doing. Foundations seem all right. The bricks could do with a bit of pointing, but I'll get round to that presently. Same as the roof, the tiles ain't bad. No, I can't see much really wrong. Of course, it looks bad as it is now, but what can you expect, with the Navy in it for a bit, then the kids breaking in and fairly wrecking the place, and the land mine what went off down on the flats. Time I get round to slapping on a bit of colour, though . . ."

We plied him with questions. Would he stay on to work for us if we bought the house? And how long did he reckon it would take? And how much was it likely to cost?

"Yes, that's all right," he replied, after a few moments of reflection. "I don't mind staying on to see the job through. I'm on me own, of course, and I'm seventy-eight, but I can do it so long as I'm not hurried. It's a good three months' work, I should say. Then there's the plumbing and so on. I've had the water turned on downstairs, but there's something wrong up in the bathroom. I'm not much of a hand at plumbing; reckon somebody would have to come and see to that. Same as the electric lighting and gas. That would have to be fixed. Better be half make the doctor an offer when I've got the place something like decent."

"But he won't sell once it's finished," I explained.

"That's true," Mr. Mellor agreed "no more he won't. I reckoned all along he wasn't keen on selling. What price was he talking of?"

We told him and he shook his head dubiously.

"He must've put his price up. Time was he only wanted £950 and all done up."

"How long ago was that?"

"Only last winter."

"There you are, you see," Dorothy broke in triumphantly. "You can't expect anything else now the war's over here. All house prices are going up."

But the old chap still looked troubled. "It's a lot of money, all the same. Just goes to prove what I've been saying all along. Things are worse now than they were during the war."

81

I made discreet inquiries at the Admiralty as to the probable duration of my leave. Six weeks appeared not unlikely.

"That's fine!" exclaimed Dorothy, as soon as she heard. "Now we'll be able to buy 'The Nore' without any haggling and get in by the winter."

"I don't quite follow," I murmured, rather overcome.

"Well, silly, if Mr. Mellor could finish the house by himself in three months, how long should it take three of us working on it?"

I knew nothing about bricks and mortar and house repairs, but a sailor can usually turn his hand to most things. Besides, we should have Mr. Mellor for guide and mentor.

"You'd better sit down right away and think out a nice, pleasant letter to tell the doctor we'd like the house."

"But what about the money?" I protested feebly.

Dorothy laughed scornfully, and set the typewriter before me. "You get on with the letter. Don't you worry about the money; the bank manager told me he'd look after that for us if ever we wanted to buy a house. Come on!"

In the end I produced a letter which I handed to Dorothy. She read it in silence.

"Well?" I asked, "will it do?"

For reply, Dorothy thrust a pen in my hand. "Sign it, quick. Now give me the envelope. I'm taking no chances; I'm posting this myself."

We waited for a week. Dorothy could scarcely sleep at night; we both lay awake pondering. Would we be lucky? Did he really mean he'd sell, or had he committed himself to others?

At last came the envelope, addressed in a thin, spidery handwriting.

"Open it," Dorothy commanded. "I can't bear it."

I smiled wryly, and moistened my lips with the tip of my tongue.

"Whittingham Hospital.
"13/8/45.

"Dear Commander Bennett,
"Thank you for your interesting letter . . ."

"Well, that's something, at any rate," I exclaimed. "I wasn't too happy about that letter."

82

" Get on with it," Dorothy urged.

" . . . Your explanations appeal to me, and I feel that you and your wife have ideals greatly in harmony with my own—so that if you have ' The Nore,' I should feel there was a kindly host and hostess—to say nothing of the little girl at the tiller—to welcome me for a cup of tea if I wanted to bathe from my old foreshore! "

" Then he's letting us have it? "

" Who's interrupting now? There's more yet. You'll probably have to promise to be a vegetarian! "

" I'd even do that if I had to. Go on! "

" . . . Yes, freehold and the usual rights of a house on a sea front to all ingress and egress.

" Yes, if you want ' The Nore ' please write a formal acceptance of my price and the usual 10 per cent. deposit, and I will pass on to my solicitors.

" I ask for this because I want to be able to give both a reason and a definite reply to two very attractive applicants who want a long lease at a good rental, and who offer to reserve my ' cabin room ' for my use. Please therefore reply to me here at once, as I shall be leaving on the 17th.

" Yours sincerely,
" (Sgd.) JOSIAH OLDFIELD,
" Lt.-Colonel, R.A.M.C."

" Well," I said, as I passed the letter over, " so that's that."
But Dorothy was far away. I recognized the symptoms. She was daydreaming—dreaming of the new kitchen to be, the distemper for the walls, the new paint, the balcony, the side wall and pointing; she was already scheming for a gas cooker and water heater, new bath and sink—a thousand-and-one ideas.

" Come on," I urged.

" Well," she began, in a matter-of-fact voice, " I was just thinking . . ."

CHAPTER VIII

"A SHIP HAS BEEN FIXED . . ."

I CAME out of the Navy in October. Meantime, we had started work on "The Nore," with old Mr. Mellor doing most of the making good; plastering walls, fitting banister rails, glazing windows, repairing fireplaces and so on. I was an utter novice at this sort of work and had to learn and lend a hand where I could, while Dorothy stripped old paper from the walls, cleared away rubbish and scrubbed endlessly day after day.

We fitted a deep sink in Dorothy's new kitchen, and brought back *June's* wash-basin for the bathroom. Then a plumber was persuaded to work evenings to complete the job. Dorothy found a nearly new gas stove which folk had been hoarding in an outhouse throughout the war. We were lucky, too, to get an electric heater for the bath; the electrician happened to be a salt-water fisherman and took on the job of rewiring in spite of pressing work elsewhere, just because the view across the bay appealed to him.

All this, and more, took less than a month. Then we started decorating. Cream was the dominant *motif*; cream paint and distemper, with dark stained floors. Mr. Mellor was amazed at the way Dorothy worked; she had practice enough in the old days painting and tarring *June*.

The fine weather held right through the autumn. Elizabeth ran in and out clad only in a bathing dress. She and Mr. Mellor became fast friends with that natural affinity between young and old; she even picked up his everlasting song: "*My mother said*"—long pause—"*I never should . . . play with the gipsies . . . in the wood.*" We came to bless it after a while, but so long as he sang to himself he was perfectly happy. Then one day while Dorothy and I worked upstairs he suddenly stopped, then started muttering to himself.

We looked at each other, brushes in hand.

"D'you think we'd better see what's the matter?" Dorothy asked.

"Coo! Dear, oh, dear!" the old chap exclaimed.

We dashed downstairs. There in the basement stood Mr. Mellor steadfastly gazing at a trickle of water emerging from the wall and slowly spreading over the floor.

He turned and peered at us over his glasses. "Can't make it out at all!"

I went outside. It was a high spring tide; there was a fresh breeze from the north-west, with seas breaking heavily on the beach. Although not reaching the house, it was obviously the sea water that was seeping through the shingle and somehow finding its way into the basement. The tide had yet another twenty minutes to flow, and the trickle soon increased to a steady flow. We tackled the flood with cans and buckets. Soon we had to roll up our trousers, and all the while our neighbours stood on their balcony admiring the white-crested seas rolling in across the bay and the small boats jumping about on their moorings.

But they, too, were soon running about with buckets. Indeed, they were worse off than ourselves, for their kitchen was in the basement, and presently they sent for the fire engine to pump out.

Meantime, we fought a losing battle with the buckets. There was nearly a foot of water over the concrete floor. But when the tide turned, to our amazement the flood waters began to drop and finally disappeared, with only a baby crab to mark its going. Later we learned that the houses along the sea wall were so constructed as to allow water to drain away, while the ground floor had been kept some three feet above the wall to ensure that the main part of the house was untouched.

The gas inspector told us of a famous band leader who once stayed at "The Nore," and whose mother went down the winding lower stairs in the early morning to make her darling son a cup of tea, when suddenly she found herself up to her waist in water, whereupon Dorothy congratulated herself for insisting on moving the kitchen to the ground floor. Luckily such high tides are few and far between. Anyway, we have only once been flooded since.

We decided on cream and dark green for the outside woodwork, though Dorothy later insisted on blue. Mr. Mellor

watched me climb the ladder to paint the eaves and decided to do them himself.

"I don't reckon it's safe for you," he said, and up he went, he who was nearly eighty!

Meantime, I built up the derelict balcony with driftwood collected from the beach, then tackled the partly demolished side wall, using stone ballast from a smack that had driven ashore and broken up at the foot of a breakwater some years before. At last we completed the top room, fitting plaster boards to the sloping ceiling. I started that job myself, offering up and holding the board with one hand and attempting to nail with the other. Elizabeth watched me in silence for a while, then went clattering downstairs.

"Mummy, mummy," she called, "do come quick! Daddy's saying such lovely things! "

At last we moved in. Luckily our furniture, which had been in store at Conyer all the war, fitted in quite well, though we were short of many things. In place of chairs for the table, we built in corner lockers that had come from *June's* galley. We had to improvise for curtaining, for we had none aboard *June*. We had to make do with stair pads instead of carpet; lamp shades we made from charts; doormats from old rope.

It was a great joy having all our books and half-forgotten treasures out once more; barge models, pictures, tools and odds and ends; practically everything had survived, thanks to the owls that haunt the old loft at Conyer and keep the mice down.

Towards the end of November I lothfully shook out the mothballs from my pre-war suits and had the seams let out a trifle. I was not enamoured of City life, for business was slack, with British shipping still very much Government-controlled. For months I felt the urge to get afloat again, yet there were times that first winter when I lay awake at night listening to the howl of the north-westerly and the roar of seas breaking on the beach, and grudgingly admitted that a landlubber's life had something to commend it after all.

And it was good to meet old friends on the Baltic Exchange again. Gradually I settled down. After all, working ships on the market is the next best thing to sailing in them.

It was surprising how soon those of us back from the Services

fell into the old ways of chartering agents with cargoes to
offer, and shipbrokers with ships to fix. Even the jargon was
unchanged.

"*THE BALTIC, Thursday.—Fairly active conditions continued to rule in the homeward chartering trades. . . . There
was sustained inquiry for Australian grain. . . .*" So ran one
market report.

And next day . . .

"Good morning, sir," said the silk-hatted attendant, standing
in the vestibule of the Baltic Mercantile and Shipping Exchange, a sturdy figure with twinkling eyes and the unmistak-
able stamp of the Navy.

I returned his greeting and passed through the swing doors
at the same time as a burly Scot who had overtaken me on the
steps. Already there was quite a crowd on the Floor—tramp
owners and brokers, merchants and chartering agents, repre-
sentative principals and chartering clerks—some bare-headed,
others in overcoats, with hands stuffed in their pockets.

"Well," said Sandy. "And how's trade to-day? Doing all
the fixtures?" He pulled out a notebook from his hip pocket.
"I suppose your barley is still there?"

"That's right. Barley in bags from South Australia for
January."

"And what's the money?"

"About 100/-. What are you thinking of?"

"Well, we've got the *Spithead* going down with phosphate.
She could give 10th January readiness in the south."

I shook my head. There was no chance at that time of a
licence to the Continent for a British ship. "Well," I said, "if
she wants to come home why not bring her on for wheat to
the U.K.?"

"Aye. For account of the Ministry of Food, no doubt. We'll
have to look into that."

He smiled, and made way for an elderly, white-haired man,
with a neatly rolled umbrella on his arm. I was turning to
greet him when a young clerk dashed up, book in hand.

"Any change, sir?" he demanded.

I shook my head and off he went.

Old Sam watched him go. "It's nice to be young, isn't it?"
he said wistfully. "You know he reminds me of the very first

man I met on the Baltic here after I came back from the Ministry at the end of the war. Just a youngster—complete stranger to me, too. 'Any change to-day, sir?' he said. Took the wind out of my sails for a moment, but I didn't want to upset him, so I just said, 'No change,' and off he buzzed quite happily. Never set eyes on him before or since."

Sam flashed a cheery smile. "That's all by the way, though I often wonder who he was. Now, then, how's Australia? We'll have our *Turtle Beach* down that way early February . . ."

Walking round the Floor, I came up with one broker after another. Each had his own distinctive mode of approach. A few were serious-minded and confined their remarks strictly to business; others were merely keeping in touch with the market. There was the usual chit-chat of fixtures and licences, news of strikes and crop prospects, port congestion and the like. These brokers had already been the rounds, and I learned among other things that the French were likely to be buying wheat again from Australia.

Alex came up in his usual quiet, imperturbable manner. "Any fresh dollar freight to-day, Benny?"

Dollars are the cabling agents' eternal quest, for American tonnage will not accept sterling. It is an exacting and often disappointing job, working the cables, nor is it always easy to reconcile American methods with our own professional code, based largely on the unwritten law.

Shortly after the war Alex had occasion to call his American office to book on a point of business ethics, only to have the terse cabled rejoinder: "*Concerned brokerages, not ethics.*"

Alex was bare of January vessels. "There's the *Moses Michael* for early February, but she'd be too late for you, I suppose?"

The other cabling agents were much the same; there were plenty of American and Canadian vessels showing up, but only for later positions. There was tonnage on passage from the River Plate to India and shortly becoming available, if only owners could be persuaded to drop down in ballast to Australia.

The Greek s.s. *Limos* was one. I tackled her owner, but he

17a "Goldsmith's *Scot* dropped down on the evening tide and brought up just above us."

P.A.M. discharging stone at Mersea Strood, with a cheerful gang of Ukrainians.

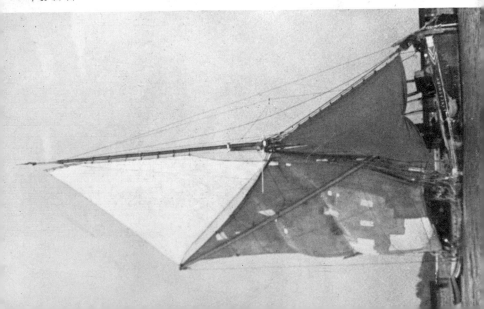

18a
Lancashire
sailing out
from Alres-
ford Creek.

b
" Now
jest you
listen
'ere . . ."

19 On the Buoy.

20 Tide time at Rochester.

21*a* *Paglesham* waiting to lock out, with topsail headstick dropped

b Waiting for tide time in the docks. *Leofleda*, wheat laden, for East Mills, Colchester, with Captain Sheldrick standing by the mast case.

22*a* Towing through Canada Dock.

  b Our steamer, the *Elkanah Crowell*, forces a passage.

23a In the Albion Dock.

b Warping alongside.

24a Waiting for our parcel.

b . . . but it w
some way dow
the forward stac

c Seven four, six threes and a couple o' twos.

only smiled and took my arm and strolled with me round the
Floor.

"You make it Western Australia loading," he said, "and
we might be interested at something like 105/-. But you know,
barley isn't the ideal cargo for her. She's a Liberty ship. Wheat,
yes, for she'd load her deadweight of heavy grain, but with
barley stowing at 58 cubic feet to the ton, why, she'd only load
about 8,300 tons. Still, we'll see."

Presently, with a fair idea of the market, though without
firm offers of tonnage, I went downstairs to join the usual
coterie for coffee. The Baltic coffee room has much to commend it in spite of its coffee. It was crowded, as usual, between
eleven and twelve o'clock, and I had to pass the table where
the group who represented my grain charterers sat in morning
conference. One leaned back and beckoned.

"Anything showing up yet for barley?"

I shook my head. "The market's quite firm, and I'm not
pushing it too much. British tonnage is out of the question
just now, of course."

"What about a Scandinavian or Greek, then?"

"There are several up in India, but 100/- doesn't seem to
tempt them. Are things really on the move?"

He looked round the table. "Well, we've just been talking
things over. There's a pretty good inquiry from the Continent
this morning, and we think we should put something out firm
if we can."

"What are the chances of dollars?" I asked. "We might
get an American at nineteen dollars—prepaid, of course.
Might even shade it a trifle."

"The Belgians should be able to put up a dollar freight.
Anyway, see if you can get a January boat in hand."

Most of the crowd at our own table were connected with the
Australian trade in one form or other. The two irrepressibles
were indulging in their regular morning wisecrack. Apparently one had telephoned the other at his home late the previous
evening.

"Yes, Benny. I caught him out properly. 'Cables and Wire
less here!' I said. 'Urgent cable for you from Australia.' He
didn't want to take it at first; he thought it was a leg-pull or

89

something, but I pretty soon had him chasing around after pencil and paper."

The victim added to the general amusement. "And there was me in my nightshirt, with that blighter rattling off *Y yellow, U uncle, Z zebra*, till I didn't know my —— from my elbow! "

Presently, another of the cabling agents came over to our table and stood behind my chair, jingling cash in his pocket.

"D'you want me, Dick? " I asked.

"When you're ready."

"I'm coming up now. Who wants my money? "

We tossed in the traditional manner, with the odd men putting their sixpences in the kitty.

"Five heads and three tails. That's me finished."

I got up, leaving the winner to settle for the coffee, and followed Dick upstairs on to the Floor.

"I hope you've got your fixing boots on to-day," he began. "I've brought a Yank along for your barley."

"Good! What's she look like? "

"Well, she's more or less on your terms. Wants dollars, of course."

We sat down at one of the tables at the side of the Exchange, while I wrote down the offer.

" s.s. *James T. Golightly*,

    9,000 tons 10% more or less,

    1st/20th January (Expected ready about 4th January),

    One port South Australia/One safe port Bordeaux/Hamburg Range,

    $19.00 Barley in bags,

    Freight prepaid New York on signing Bills of Lading,

    600 tons per day load @ current rate,

    Customary discharge,

    $1,500 demurrage, $500 despatch,

    'Austral' Charter Party,

    $2\frac{1}{2}$% commission,

    Usual American Clauses."

"That's the lot," said Dick. "It's up to you now."

I sat back for a few moments. "Of course, he's a bit out on terms. We'd have to have the usual two ports load in South Australia. They can only manage 500 tons a day, too."

"You can come back on those points. That's not going to stand in the way of a fixture."

"Rate's a bit high, too," I continued. "D'you think there's much give in him?"

"I've got no discretion, if that's what you mean," he said, and we both laughed.

"And how long can we have the offer?"

"Let's see. I've got it firm for reply in New York noon Monday, and they're six hours behind us. We'll make it three o'clock Monday. That'll give you the week-end to work on it."

I slipped down to join my principals, who looked up expectantly.

"Well, now, what have you got for us?"

I smiled, and lay the offer on the table.

"That looks all right to me," one of them said at last, leaning back in his chair. "What d'you think?"

I shrugged my shoulders. "The rate's not out of the way. You'll want the usual loading terms, of course. I must admit the market's quite steady and there's nothing much else to get our teeth into."

"Righto, we'll work on this . . . We'll have to get Antwerp into line . . . and cable Australia, too."

*   *   *   *   *

The next morning was Saturday, and things were quiet on the Baltic. Then, quite by chance, I gathered that the French were likely to be in the market on Monday for January tonnage. I telephoned my principals, but they had no news.

"That lets me out, then," said Dick presently, when he joined me on the Floor. "I want to slip off. I'm going way down in the country for the week-end. You've got the ship in hand till Monday, so you won't want me."

Twenty minutes later, just as I was going off, too, my name was called from the rostrum.

"Local line, please, sir."

Charterers were on the telephone. Would I wait for them? They were coming over right away. It transpired they now had the barley in hand as well as a bid from Antwerp buyers, which enabled them to sell and charter.

"We'll accept the *James T. Golightly,*" they decided. "We

91

want her and can't afford to mess about, so if you can get her on our terms we won't grumble about the rate."

I dashed off to telephone Dick.

"I'm awfully sorry, sir," came the reply, "but they've all gone from the Chartering Department."

Normally I could have contacted Dick at home, but with him away there was nothing for it but to leave things over the week-end. It was unfortunate, for, as my charterers pointed out, although we *should* be able to get buyers to renew their bid, the barley market might be right off on Monday. What worried me more, though, was the fact that we might expect more competition on the freight side next week.

* * * * *

Sure enough there were complications on Monday morning.

Dick was soon on the telephone. "I hear you wanted me Saturday," he began. "What was it—clean confirmation?"

"Not quite, but there wasn't much between us."

"Well, you're still within your time. I'll get you a reply this afternoon."

"Sorry, Dick, but I can't make you a bid just at present. There's a snag cropped up this morning over the dollar credit."

Dick's silence was impressive. "That's a devil," he said at last. "What's the form going to be?"

"Well, my folk are trying to get things ironed out. They're quite hopeful, but we just can't say anything till then."

"All right, Ben. We'll have to hope for the best. I'll see you on the Floor."

I went across to the Baltic rather earlier than usual to get round the market. The French, of course, were open Australia / Marseilles for much the same position as ourselves. Obviously, Dick would soon hear of the order, but meantime we could do nothing but wait.

Lunch-time came, and still no news. At five o'clock I had to tell Dick there was nothing further to be done that day. I longed to ask whether he was working with the French, but discretion prompted me to restrain my impatience. It was pointless putting ideas into his head.

* * * * *

Tuesday morning I met Dick on the Floor as usual.

"Any news?"

92

"Not yet. Hullo! That sounds like me being called."

I was wanted down below in the coffee room, where charterers were grouped around the table in earnest discussion.

They had the bid in hand again, with a credit arranged to cover the dollar freight.

"You know," said one, "I think we ought to take the *James T. Golightly.*"

"As she stands?" I demanded.

"Well, we'd like to get our usual terms, of course, but as far as the rate is concerned, we've already agreed to pay the nineteen dollars."

"True enough, but we never made the offer."

"So what?"

"Well, this is how I see it," he said slowly. "I admit the market's firm, but the French have been in the market now since yesterday morning, and if the *James T. Golightly* meant to switch to them, she'd have done so by now. No, seeing you've got Antwerp buyers behind you for a couple of days, why not give her the nineteen dollars for Bordeaux/Hamburg Range, but knock off fifty cents for Antwerp or Rotterdam?"

"Mmm. And there's nothing else showing up, you say?"

"Not so far. Still, Antwerp or Rotterdam discharge is worth half a dollar to any owner."

They thought it over for a few moments, then gave me their blessing, and a final admonition not to lose the ship. "You'd better pad your trousers if you miss her!" was their parting shot.

*　　　*　　　*　　　*　　　*

I sensed who it was coming through on the telephone soon after ten o'clock next day.

"Is that you, Ben? We've got our cable in." Dick paused, and all the doubts and hopes of the past few days crystallized in a single flutter of apprehension. It seemed an eternity before he continued: "It's short and sweet. He accepts your offer."

So that was that! Jubilation rapidly gave way to a sense of anti-climax. We ran quickly through the terms. Everything was in order.

"By the way," I said, "what's happening to the French?"

"Why, we've got the *John G. Trent* under offer to them."

"Have you, by Jove? I didn't even know you had another ship. Where's she suddenly sprung from?"

"Oh," said Dick, with such an air of innocence that I could picture him at the other end of the phone with his tongue in his cheek. "My owner's got the pair of 'em in much the same position. Didn't I tell you?"

*   *   *   *   *

Next day the market report ran as follows: —

"*THE BALTIC, Tuesday.—The freight market maintained a good tone, and rates were fully steady. . . . In the Australian section a ship has been fixed. . . . Another is believed to be closely treating. . . .*"

*   *   *   *   *

Times have changed in 1949. There is still bulk buying of foodstuffs and chartering of tramp tonnage by the Ministry of Food, but British vessels may now trade freely in the world markets. The essence of chartering and shipbroking—the friendliness and mutual trust that go to the making of a fixture —all these things remain the same. And since the war I have had the joy of fixing some of the few remaining four-masted barques with grain from Australia: *Passat, Lawhill, Viking, Pamir.*

There is romance yet in shipping!

CHAPTER IX

DOWN SWIN AGAIN

ONE week-end towards the end of June, 1946, we borrowed *Nancy Grey* and sailed her from Upnor to Whitstable and nosed her in over the flats to a mooring off "The Nore." Elizabeth came paddling out in great excitement, clutching her frock in one hand and shoes in the other, with Dorothy following close behind. *Nancy Grey*—10-ton, 30-ft. barge-yacht—was ours for a fortnight.

Monday was fair, with the wind westerly and rather too much of it for comfort, so we stored ship and gave her a scrub at low water. We were hoping to get down Swin again for the first time since the war. But there was no hurry; this was Elizabeth's first cruise, and our plans turned largely on the weather.

Strangely enough, on board that night for the first time, it was Elizabeth who slept while Dorothy and I lay awake in our bunks listening to the wind in the rigging and all the multifarious small-boat noises and creakings we had almost forgotten over the war years. I turned out once to secure the halyards from flapping against the mast, and again to tauten the tiller lashing, and yet again in a vain attempt to stop the leeboards from clattering.

Soon after midnight *Nancy Grey* took the ground, and in spite of her shoal draft, she bumped and shuddered. After a while the lapping of the waves died down and the gurgling under the bottom ceased.

"Are you awake, Dorothy?" I called softly.

"Yes. How long before we float again?"

"About a couple of hours."

There was silence for a while. Neither of us was looking forward to the flood, with the prospect of lying between wind and tide.

"Now's the time," I murmured. "That is, if you really want to go."

It did seem rather silly lying awake out there when we had perfectly good beds waiting for us ashore, so we wrapped Elizabeth in a blanket, and made our way over the flats to our house on the sea wall.

By morning the westerly had blown itself out, but it was Elizabeth's fifth birthday, and we decided to stay ashore for her party.

We went aboard again that night, though, and slept soundly. It was a fine morning when I turned out at seven o'clock, with a light southerly breeze and a mist over the marshes. I lit the Calor gas stove for a cup of tea, and went up on deck. Soon Dorothy and Elizabeth came tumbling out. Over went our mooring buoy. A tug on the jib sheet and we were away. Once clear of the anchorage, up went mainsail and staysail, both dressed, barge-fashion, with fish oil and red ochre.

With a fair wind and two hours of the flood to run, we reached out past the Columbine and up to the Spile Buoy. Then we bore away across the Estuary, with Warden Point astern half shrouded in the mist, and the Great Nore Towers over the port bow.

A smart motor-cruiser coming down the Thames altered course towards us. We were on the gybe, and I was not too happy at the thought of them crossing our bows. But they only wanted to speak us, and came ranging up on our quarter.

A man with glasses slung round his neck emerged from the wheelhouse and clambered up on the foredeck.

"We're lost," he shouted. "Can you tell us the way to Margate?"

Dorothy and I looked at each other in amazement.

"We've just come up from the Spile," I replied. "There she lies about a couple of miles astern. Bears about south-south-east."

The motor cruiser moved off slowly. Possibly the group of buoys which I took to be radar navigation buoys bewildered them.

"How ridiculous!" Dorothy exclaimed. "I wouldn't mind betting they've got old pre-war charts."

"Like ours," I murmured. "Last correction June, 1933!"

Navigation during the war became a serious matter for many of us, yet here we were reverting to type, with out-of-date

96

charts and primitive instruments. We are all tarred with the same brush—most of us, anyway.

Dorothy caught my eye, and we both laughed.

There was the usual stream of traffic passing up and down the Thames. A Polish steamer lay hove-to off the forts . . . a sailing barge was coming out from the Medway . . . somehow, though, there was an unfamiliar air about the whole scene. Maybe it was we missed the Nore Light Vessel, which was always such a focal point in the Thames Estuary.

The Mouse, too, was missing, but down S.W. Reach, with the Blacktail Spit and the Measured Mile Beacons, the S.E. Maplin and all the rest of them, and with a couple of barges beating up along the edge of the sands, things were much more as we remembered them in the old days. A mine exploding somewhere over by the Barrow Deep was the only disturbing element.

At the Whitaker Beacon, with the usual cormorant perched on the topmark, we had to make up our minds whether to make for Burnham River or carry on down Swin. I was rather keen to make a fair wind of it for Battlesbridge. But it was a fair wind, too, for Pin Mill.

Dorothy thought it over. " I think we'd better push on while we can. You'll want to get to Pin Mill sooner or later, I know. We'd get in before dark, I suppose? "

It seemed safe enough on the face of things. The time was only two o'clock, and we had another couple of hours of the ebb with us yet, so we ran on past the Whitaker Buoy, and the barge we had noticed coming out of the Medway gradually overhauled us. She was the *Pudge*—a veteran of Dunkirk— under power and with only her topsail set. She was not to run away from us yet awhile, for she grounded in the Wallet Spitway, and so did a smart staysail schooner. A barge-yacht like *Nancy Grey* scores in shoal waters. We came through the Spitway from the Bell Buoy to the Wallet Buoy without even the leeboards touching.

There were barges rounding the Naze and bound up Swin for London River. These Ipswich barges are probably as well found as any these days, and *Dannebrog* and *Spinaway C,* with Cranfield's white ball in their topsails, made a grand sight beating through the Wallet. Elizabeth stood and waved,

97

and the skipper of the *Spinaway C,* stooping to peer beneath
the foot of his mainsail, turned and gave her a cheery greeting.

We lost the tide off Frinton, but the big reaching jib brought
us along in fine style past Walton Pier. There were storm
clouds gathering over the land, and just when Elizabeth and
I were trying to salvage a wooden packing case, the wind
suddenly died on us. We whistled, and presently a puff came
out of the south-west, which brought us along almost to the
Naze. Then the thunderstorm broke and the heavens opened.
The land was completely blotted out. We were in a world
of our own, cut off by a curtain of white as the rain bounced
feet high from the water in a perfect frenzy. Then came more
catspaws and more rain until at last the true breeze persisted
from the north-east.

We trimmed our sheet and tried short boards close inshore
and made longer boards out to the Stone Banks . . . still
we hung abreast the Naze. This plug to windward over a foul
tide at the end of a long day was beginning to pall. Elizabeth
was getting tired, and Dorothy had visions of anchoring outside
for the night.

" Better start up the engine," she suggested.

As I had feared, it came to that, but it was nine o'clock
before we crept round Stone Point. The tide was done, and we
brought up just inside.

Next morning we took the last of the flood up to the anchorage by the Twizzle, and spent the day in Walton, sailing the
dinghy up the creek to the yacht club hard. Elizabeth enjoyed
her run ashore, eating vast quantities of ice cream and in-
veigling us to the fair, where Dorothy and I had to share in
the dubious pleasures of swings and roundabouts.

Elizabeth was all for going ashore again in the morning,
until we persuaded her that Pin Mill also had its attractions,
and got away to a slashing easterly breeze.

The wind was piping up as we threshed across Dovercourt
Bay, and we had to make a couple of boards before we could
clear the breakwater, now just awash. Then we eased our sheets
and sped across Harwich Harbour for the Orwell. Harwich
seemed unusually bare of shipping, though there was plenty
up Parkeston way, and a whole bunch of corvettes laid up on
Shotley Spit, with their bows overhanging the saltings.

The corn was ripening at Levington, and there were poppies in the field where the path led uphill from the tumbledown wharf at the head of the creek. We toyed with the idea of anchoring *Nancy Grey* off the entrance and sailing up in the dinghy, but the breeze was piping up all the time, so we ran on for Pin Mill and brought up at the lower end of the anchorage.

In the old days we invariably seemed to come in from sea with a blustering sou'wester to a blessed haven of peace and quiet round Collimer Point. To-day, though, there was no shelter; we lay athwart the ebb and sailed round and round our anchor in the fierce rain squalls. After awhile we weighed and ran up-river under jib to a quieter berth above the hard.

Ashore it was the Pin Mill of old. The little lad in seaboots and peaked cap no longer tended the dinghies, but his young brother had taken over from him. There was a yacht up for a scrub, and the sailing barge *Water Lily* repairing on the hard. The "Butt and Oyster" still opened, albeit at eight o'clock.

The next day we took the bus to Ipswich, where the good folk were still mopping up water after a cloudburst, and clearing away mud from their garden paths. As usual, we found the docks a great attraction. The old-time miscellaneous collection of odds and ends of craft was no longer in evidence, but there were still plenty of sailing barges, and Elizabeth was much intrigued at the mills, where flour was being unloaded from one barge, going up through a trap-door and to all intents and purposes emerging a little further along to come sliding down a chute into the hold of another barge.

We strolled along the quayside past the Customs House to the ship-chandlers, where I bought canvas to re-cover a life-buoy and some cotton line for beckets.

There is an air of affluence about Ipswich. It is a market town and seaport abounding in old buildings, yet keeping abreast of the times. The shops seem to specialize in their own particular line, and are something more than mere stores. As for lunch, maybe it was that excellent meal that served to colour our impressions of Ipswich. Elizabeth had an ice cream; Dorothy enjoyed her shopping, and we returned to Pin Mill well laden and very cheerful.

Sunday was blustery but fine, with the wind westerly

and rather too much for a comfortable passage up the coast. We stayed in our snug berth and watched the local craft get under way, very soon to be joined by the Ipswich boats— yachts, motor cruisers, dinghies, and a small, open steam launch, whose crew received a rapturous welcome from Elizabeth.

Early next morning we slipped quietly down river on the ebb. The sun was beginning to break through the showers and lit up the fields of corn, now sadly battered after the rain storms of the past few days.

There was the usual small fleet of barges at Shotley. Our old friend, the *Pudge,* was among them. Apparently the barge skippers had little faith in the weather and were waiting for a slant up Swin to London River and the Medway.

A little sloop anchored close inshore was weighing, and there were sweepers on their way out, too. We cut across their wake and carried a fair breeze out to the Naze. It was beginning to freshen, and we hove-to in the slack water under the shelter of the land to take down a couple of rolls in the mainsail.

The sloop coming up astern was just able to lay up along the coast, but the best we could do in *Nancy Grey* was a long leg and a short, sailing full all the time, punching the short, steep seas of the weather-going tide. We spoke her as we crossed tacks. She was making for Bradwell, and stood on for the Knoll, but we came about again for the Inner Bench Head and the Colne.

Suddenly Elizabeth spotted a toy yacht heading bravely for the open sea. We luffed up quickly and tried to pick it up, but we were too late. Dorothy was all for pushing on; she was hungry and refused to go below until we were brought up. But Elizabeth was most upset.

"I haven't got a little boat of my own. *Do* get it for me."

We tried again, gybing this time and laying up close-hauled. I jammed the tiller hard down and left Dorothy to it while I dashed forward with a short boathook. Alas, we were short!

"That's enough," exclaimed Dorothy.

"Just once more," Elizabeth pleaded, and dashed into the cabin to bury her head in the bunk cushions. "Don't say anything if you can't get it. Just don't say anything at all."

100

Another gybe, and I jilled her up to windward, then left the tiller to Dorothy and clambered up on the foredeck.

"Luff on her!"

We lost way. I reached down with the boathook. Our bows lifted. Crunch! The bow wave set the boat off just out of reach. It was too bad. Then, to my amazement, the little boat suddenly gybed over and came sailing down towards us.

Elizabeth was still kneeling in the cabin, with her hands over her ears and her feet drumming on the floor. She could hardly believe her eyes when I handed the trim little blue and white craft down the hatch.

Brightlingsea Creek looked as full as ever with yachts and laid-up naval craft, so we held on for the Pyefleet and brought up just inside. Elizabeth was very tired and soon went to sleep with her boat propped by her side.

We lay in Pyefleet for several days waiting for the weather to fine up. Elizabeth was quite happy, for she found a children's playground on Westmarsh Point at Brightlingsea, with swings and roundabouts. But we missed the pre-war oyster dredgers, and only one small yacht came into our anchorage, and she went well up the creek. We missed the river police, too, with their local news and gossip.

The marsh birds were still in their thousands on the saltings. There were barges, too, working up and down the Colne. Goldsmith's *Cambria* dropped down on the ebb and brought up just off the Pyefleet Spit Buoy. She was steel built and deep-laden with sand for London River.

The next morning we turned out to find *Cambria* away. The breeze had dropped a little—so we thought—and at half ebb we rolled three reefs in the mainsail and got under way for Burnham.

Elizabeth was disappointed at leaving the swings.

"Where's Burnham?" she demanded.

"Out there," I replied, pointing down river. "Straight on and second to the right."

"That's a funny place. Are there any swings there?"

"Sure to be, and slides, too, I expect."

"Goody, goody!" And with that she went back to her crayons.

Outside, though, we found all the wind we wanted, and somewhere by the Knoll *Nancy Grey* caught a succession of

101

steep, breaking seas on the bluff of her bow that knocked the way completely off her.

" What's happening? " Dorothy demanded as she looked out of the hatch. " We'd better turn back if it's going to be like this."

" It's all right," I said cheerfully. " We'll find things a bit quieter in the Rays'n."

Just then we slammed into another hollow sea.

" Look out! " I yelled, as a burst of spray came flying over the cabin top.

It was too late. Dorothy shook the water out of her hair and looked at me reproachfully. There was nothing else to do but to give in gracefully and run back.

All this time Elizabeth had been busy with her crayons, balancing herself on her knees, with her head touching the floor. Now she looked up and wanted to know why we were not going to Burnham.

" It's too rough."

" But I want to go on the swings," she declared, and her lips dropped.

" Well, we'll take you ashore at Brightlingsea again if you're good."

" All right," and with barely a glance at the white-flecked seas she went happily back to her crayons.

On the way we came up with *Cambria* creeping in under staysail, foresail and mizzen. Somewhere out by the Spitway the joggle end of her sprit had carried away, bringing down mainsail and topsail. She had to make a couple of slow, laborious trips before she brought up under the lee of Mersea Point.

Later in the day more barges dropped down the Colne and anchored. George Blake, the young skipper of the *P.A.M.*, was a friend from pre-war days when he sailed as mate with his father in Wakeley's *Fanny* and later in the *Southwark*. He wanted to know what had happened to *June*.

We told him she was finished and that we were living at Whitstable.

" That's a pity. Dad was asking after you. He's got the *Lancashire* now. Reckon you'd better come away with us for a trip just to keep your hand in."

102

I laughed. "That's a good idea, George. And so I will next summer. What d'you make of the weather?"

"I don't go much on it. Never know, though, it might no'ther out."

Time was getting on. We wanted to beach *Nancy Grey* for a scrub and a coat of anti-fouling before handing her back to the owner, so next morning, with reasonable prospects of a fine day, we decided to make for the Medway.

We were under way by six o'clock, and lay out through the Raysand Channel close-hauled on the starboard tack. The best water was said to be a cable or so off the R.A.F. target; at any rate, we found a minimum of five feet about an hour before low water.

Seven Ipswich barges came chasing over the Spitway and held on up Swin. In due course *Nancy Grey* tailed on the procession until, coming up to the Maplin Spit Buoy, Dorothy noticed a swirl of sandy water close under the starboard bow. The flood was beginning to make; it might well have been a wreck. Hurriedly we bore away . . . and again from yet another unpleasant-looking patch right under our bows.

It was the Maplin Spit itself. I had not realized there was a depth of only three feet so close inside the buoy.

Away to the eastward a mine went up, but Elizabeth was much more interested in the seals basking in the sunshine on the Barrow Sands.

The wind was backing. We had a plug to windward all the way up S.W. Reach and barely saved our tide into the Medway. It had been a long day, and we were glad enough to bring up off the flats by the West Shore.

Next morning we beat up the Medway and put *Nancy Grey* on the beach at Upnor. The owner came down in the afternoon. I crawled from under the bilges, with a wet seat and plastered to the eyes with red anti-fouling. Elizabeth had been helping to stir the paint, and she, too, was well covered.

"Well," said Ralph, passing up a basket of luscious raspberries to Dorothy in the cockpit. "Have you enjoyed yourselves?"

I grinned, and started to clean myself on a handful of cotton waste.

"Yes, indeed. Almost like old times."

103

CHAPTER X

STONE FOR MERSEA STROOD

P.A.M. was loading stone for Mersea Strood in a quiet riverside berth set among the trees about halfway between Allington Locks and Maidstone.

My friend, George Blake, the fair-haired, burly young skipper, was playing with the dog on the cabin top as I came trudging along the towpath opposite, with a duffle bag slung over my shoulder. He greeted me with a broad grin and sculled the boat across, while I stood and mopped my face.

"You're looking very smart, George," I said, pointing to the grey-painted wale and gold scrollwork on the bows.

"We're not long off the ways—not that they did much to us. Couldn't get the timber."

I tossed my gear into the boat. It looked a lot, but was mostly seaboots and oilskins, for I knew how wet a barge could be deep-laden.

George laughed. "You should've known we're only fair-weather sailors." Then, as we came alongside, "That's right, Bill, ain't it?"

The mate appeared at the cabin hatch. "What's that?"

"I get sick every time it comes on to blow, don't I?"

Bill winked at me. "Not half as sick as I get sometimes."

"There you are," said George. "That's the way I get treated. No respect at all." He reached for the small black Labrador that sat watching proceedings with head cocked on one side. "That Bill o' your'n's a bad 'un, ain't he, Sheila, my little pigeon?" Then, as she muzzled into his face, George thrust her aside and roared, "Aht of it!"

Bill was quite unmoved. "There's a cup o' tea on the table."

The cabin was roomy, as barge cabins go, with light-grained woodwork and white-painted deckhead. Originally there was a small stateroom to starboard for the skipper, but the space had been given over to a large water tank.

Following the modern trend, a foot or so had been taken

from the cabin and about four feet from the hold, and a small diesel installed, but the engine was not a success and was due to be replaced by another. Meantime, George had unshipped the propeller and was sailing without a mizzen. The barge herself had been rebuilt in 1945 at a cost of £2,000, which was more than she cost new in 1901. They had made a good job of her at Limehouse, stripping her completely inside and fitting her out with new keelsons, ceiling and lining. She had been doubled, too—"put in a box," as the old bargemen would say.

We were still sitting over our tea when the men started loading again. There were two on the job, filling their wheelbarrows from a dump and trundling along a plank across ten or twelve feet of water to the barge, which lay off with inside leeboard lowered to keep her from grounding on the bank.

"I reckon it's a shame," said George. "Fancy putting a good barge like this in the stone work, and after all that's been done to her, too. You never know what sort of a berth you're getting on the sea walls. Most times we have to drive in our own posts for moorings ashore, besides laying out anchors bow and stern. The other week we got blown up the wall at Bradwell; that's why we had to go on the yard at Maldon to get our chines seen to. Same as unloading, they have to chuck up the stone on deck. Smashes up your coamings and rails something awful. There's one thing, though, stone does pay all right."

P.A.M. was loading 120 yards of stone for Mersea Strood at 9s. 6d. a yard. Towage would come to about £10, leaving a net freight of £47 to be divided equally between owner and crew in time-honoured fashion. Skipper and mate usually share in the proportion of two to one. In the case of an auxiliary barge, it is customary for the owner to pay for lubricating oil and for fuel oil to be shared equally.

George had no doubts about the life. "It's what you make of it," he said. "Money's all right, too, so long as you keep at it steady. Taking it by and large, barging's all right."

The little steam tug Knighton appeared soon after four o'clock with a couple of lighters in tow, but we were still short of a full cargo, and she went off at a steady three knots towards Allington Locks. Thirty minutes later she came back, but we were still not finished.

105
H

"How long now?" the tug master demanded.

"Want a tidy bit yet," George replied, and turned to the men who were loading. "Another twenty barrow-loads, I'd say."

"We're due to knock off in another ten minutes, Skipper."

George shrugged his shoulders and turned with his hands in his pockets. "I reckon we've had it for to-day. Pity. We could have pushed on down Chatham Reach to-night."

"And saved the week-end at the other end, I suppose?"

"I'm not worried about that, but you know what it is being stuck up here. All right for a day or two, then you want to get down out of it."

The loading woke us next morning. I poked my head out of the bunk which Bill had insisted on making over to me, and found a pot of tea on the table.

George was still in his bunk, a bleary-eyed, towsled vision in striped pyjamas. Presently he stretched out a brawny arm and lifted Sheila by the scruff of her neck. "Hullo, my little pigeon," he cooed. "And who came into my bunk during the night? I didn't half bawl at her."

I remembered dimly she had tried to snuggle down with me.

Bill was busy with Primus and frying pan. "Reckon both of you must've kicked her out, 'cos she finished up with me on the lockers."

After a while, a head looked down the hatch.

"Finished, Skipper."

George turned out and went on deck. Soon, more stone thumped aboard.

"Told 'em we wanted another six," George said as he sat down to a heaped-up plate of bacon, tomatoes and fried bread. "I reckon it's up to me to look after the gov'nor, don't you? Pretty sure if I don't, nobody else will."

High water at the locks was at six o'clock. We had all day to cover up the hatches and scrub the decks. George grew restless. For a while he sat watching the clouds and the wind in the trees, then jumped to his feet. "Come on, let's sail her down to the locks."

We cast off the shore lines and poked our bows out into the stream.

106

"Shake out the mains'l."

The breeze was patchy and fluky and at times we lay almost becalmed under the trees. Once we fouled the overhanging branches, and littered the hatch top with twigs and leaves It was a pleasant part of the river, with yachts moored along the tree-fringed grounds of Allington Castle.

P.A.M. glided gently alongside the stone wall to await her turn for locking through. The *Knighton* arrived and slipped her tow; an empty coal lighter came on to fetch up on the piling opposite with a smack that made George wince.

"Beats me how those old craft stand it," he muttered. "Well, I suppose we might as well lower away."

Bill had already run off the stayfall on the trip down river, unwinding all but the last three turns from the windlass barrel, and coiling down on the foredeck. George cast off the stopper and surged the stayfall so that mast and gear dropped aft, with the sprit overhanging the starboard quarter and the mainmast resting on an upturned plank under the lower cap.

There was the usual tide-time activity as the lock gates opened. A motor-barge gave us a tow in. The gates shut, and the lower sluices were opened. Within a few minutes we had dropped to the level of the tidal waters in the Lower Medway, where the diesel tug that had brought up a string of coal lighters was waiting.

"He's got to get the light barges through Aylesford Bridge before high water, so he won't waste much time," Bill exclaimed. "Riding light, same as they are, there's precious little room to spare in the bridge hole."

The motor-barge had gone ahead as soon as the gates opened, and it was heavy work shoving *P.A.M.* out of the lock.

"Hold on," said George, and hailed one of the lockmen: "Give us a drop o' water, mate! "

A few turns of the sluice on the upper gate set the water bubbling under our stern, and within a few seconds *P.A.M.* shot out of the lock.

"Keep on going! " shouted the tug master.

"Do you want us on the hook? " George demanded, and was answered with a shake of the head and a thumb cocked in the direction of the empty coal lighter.

107

"That's right," George replied, with a broad grin. "You'll want someone behind to keep you steady."

To be on the hook immediately abaft the tug means almost complete freedom from steering, whereas those on the tail are usually hard at it most of the time in these narrow, twisting reaches.

There was much good-natured badinage passing between the craft round the locks. One lighterman was particularly loquacious. He cursed the tug and the skipper and the world in general.

"Reckon you're the bloke what's got us lightermen a bad name," shouted one, and was met in turn with a stream of abuse.

George shrugged his shoulders. "Reckon the tug chaps turned him down for a cup o' tea. He's usually pretty lively, but he must've had one more than usual to-day."

The lines were made fast and the tug throbbed as she forged ahead over the last of the flood. She blew as Aylesford came into sight, for below the bridge is a blind turn, and upcoming craft with the tide under them have the right of way. The picturesque old bridge barely allows a light barge through the centre arch, as innumerable scores on the stonework testify.

We picked up a lighter loaded with fine sand for Dagenham just below the bridge. The river begins to broaden out here, and the tug skipper decided to double up his tow. *P.A.M.* went on the hook alongside the sand lighter, and the empty barge dropped astern.

Paper is the chief industry of the Medway valley. Cement-encrusted buildings still stand on the river banks, but their chimneys no longer belch white clouds of smoke. Gone, too, are Lee's barges with the white rampant horse of Kent painted on their sails, and all the smart little craft belonging to Peters and the West Kent and the Burham Cement Company.

There are many who would be glad to see cement smoke again in the valley; so would I if it meant barges, too.

There was another lighter waiting at Snodland. The tide was ebbing, and there was no room for the tug to swing with her tow. She just eased down while the lighter cast off from the wharf and shot out half athwart the tide.

"Have a fender ready, Bill." George had an aversion to

108

picking up lighters down tide. "Only got to get your rail under his swim and you've had it."

All went well, and we were soon under way again. Bill slipped below to make tea, and the lightermen were invited over. They were staid, decent chaps, quiet-spoken and full of river lore. After their tea they gathered round the windlass and shipped the handles—one up and the other down—and spitting on their hands, they set to work. The mast crutch fell on the hatch top. Slowly the mainmast rose, but just as the headrope tautened to the weight of the sprit, they straightened up as one man and rested against the windlass bitts, while we passed under Rochester Bridge.

Once through the bridge, there was no time for talking. It was just a slow, hard grind, turning away at the windlass to the steady *clank, clank, clank* of the pawls.

The tug rounded up off Cory's hoists, and George ran aft to cast off the lighters.

Clank, clank, clank . . . The stayfall seemed endless.

At last came the welcome cry: "Hold on. That'll do her!"

"Topm'st next," muttered Bill.

We swayed it aloft. The tug was rounding up again as I slipped aloft to ship the fid.

"Leggo, Mate!"

The sand lighter moored up, and the tug skipper looked round expectantly, pointing to the buoys off Ship Pier, where barges usually bring up. It was just after nine o'clock and half ebb.

"Nice time for a bucketful," Bill murmured, and we licked our lips wistfully.

But our skipper was made of sterner stuff. "Reckon she'd just about look down Chatham Reach. Can't tell but what it won't come flat calm in the morning, and you know what it's like round Chatham Point with the ebb setting over on the Gun Wharf. Ask him to give us a start down Chatham Reach, Bill . . ."

We set up the topmast forestay and lowered the heavy iron crosstrees into place. Then out came the topsail sheet and both of us tailed on the halyard.

"Shake out the mains'l!"

George grabbed the mainsheet block as the heavy sail unfurled, and hooked it on the traveller.

" Jib or fores'l? "

" Jib! "

The tug had fetched us round the point and slipped our towrope. We trimmed the sheets and paused for breath. It was a joy to be under sail again, free at last from the whiff of exhaust and the insidious throb of the tug's powerful diesel engine.

There was still work to be done. Our tow rope was hanging from the bows; the stopper had to be passed before the stay-fall could be run off the windlass barrel and coiled below; the anchor on the foredeck had to be manhandled overside; lines had to be flaked down on the hatch top . . .

The breeze was taking off. We fetched slowly past Upnor Castle and the *Arethusa*—once the four-masted barque *Peking,* and now a training ship—on past the yachts clustered off the old barge yard, away down to the bight under Cockham Wood.

There, in the quiet of the evening, we called it a day, and brought up to our anchor. After supper, Bill hung out the riding light; in a little while, with the small cabin lamp aglim, *P.A.M.* slept.

*   *   *   *   *

Next morning we were under way early and slipped quietly down on the ebb. I helped the mate square off the foredeck and came strolling aft, where George greeted us with a disarming smile.

" You might take the wheel for a bit, Bill."

The mate assumed an outraged expression and turned to me for support. " There he goes again. I don't know what skippers are coming to these days. Always the same. I pulls out the tawps'l sheet. Up tawps'l. That's all right. I don't mind heavin' up the anchor meself, but after I'm hove up, I've got to pull out the mainsheet, though it ain't my job by rights. Do I take it easy then? ' Take the wheel,' he says, ' while I have a smoke.' "

George was quite unperturbed and only grinned the more. " You may as well pick up the mains'l while you're at it. We'll be gybing in a minute and don't want our new sprit come tumbling down."

110

We turned to again and brailed in a few cloths of the main-sail while George bore up between the old Hoo and Darnet Forts. The sprit came lurching over.

"Slacken off yer runners. Reckon she'll hold this gybe now. Here you are, Bill. Take her."

On the flats just below the pier at Port Victoria lay the wreck of the *Arcades,* one of the finest of the sailing barges built between the wars. She was on passage from Colchester to Ridham Dock laden with straw when the mate noticed a wisp of smoke coming up from the big deck stack. The straw must have been smouldering for hours, for as soon as they tried to get at the trouble the stack caved in together with the deck and mast case. A naval tug put out from Sheerness and managed to tow her in, but she burnt out over on the West Shore.

"I don't think they did find out how it happened," said George as he took the wheel again. "Probably a cigarette end down the hold while she loaded."

There were plenty more wrecks out in the Thames Estuary; one Liberty ship with masts and upperworks showing was reputed to have several thousand tons of ammunition still on board.

"I hope we're not around when they start on her," said Bill. "There won't half be some fireworks if they try to blow her up!"

There were barges coming down Sea Reach, emerging wraith-like from the haze, and the usual procession of tramps and coasters sending their wash rolling aboard through the scuppers and setting our leeboards clattering.

Horlock's *Repertor* came up with us off the Maplin edge, a dun-coloured steel barge rigged out with steel spars and carry-ing a well-cut suit of sails. She was probably bound round to the Stour with grain for the Mistley Mills.

Motoring over the last of the ebb came *Glenway,* followed by *Beatrice Maud,* with a stack of straw six or seven bales high, and towing a sailing barge alongside. A whole fleet of barges was working through the Spitway and up Swin for London River and the Medway.

"Can't be a lot o' down tide now," said George, as we came slowly up to the N.E. Maplin Buoy. "We'll have the flood

under us up the Whitaker. I don't reckon she'll quite look up, but she'll make a long leg and a short of it."

Barges bound round for Maldon and the Colne usually favour the Whitaker Channel and the Raysand in preference to working the Swin Spitway outside the Buxey Sands. The breeze, which the sun seemed to be killing, now freshened as we turned up the Whitaker close-hauled, with leeboards lowered away. *P.A.M.* had a nice-setting suit of canvas, though George said she was due for a new topsail soon. " She gets along to wind'rd pretty fair, though I reckon she'd carry another couple o' cloths in the mains'l. Not that I'm keen on heavy gear. A fifty-six foot sprit's plenty big enough for me."

P.A.M. had just been rigged out with a new sprit. The old one lay in halves on either side of the main hatch. " Gov'nor wants it for piling or something. Gorn rotten just by the yard taickle band—Oregon pine, too. It's a wonder we hadn't got into trouble with all the wind we had early on in the year.

" Soon as we saw how bad it was I 'phoned up the gov'nor. 'Better come round to London,' he said, 'and we'll see about it.'

" 'Not me,' I says. 'You'll have to send a sprit down here, 'cos I'm not sailing on that one any more.'

" All the same, I was sorry to lose that old sprit. You know what it come off? Why Brice's *Ella and Norman* that finished up on the Maplins before the war. Owners drew the insurance money, but when we come up past in the *Southwark* not long after, Dad noticed she'd picked herself up, so he goes and sees the insurance people and gets himself the job of salvaging her. Three of us went down—me and my brother and Dad. We couldn't do anything with the barge, for she'd sat on her anchor, but we got off all the gear save the mainm'st, and we left that to mark the wreck. Fifteen quid each, they gave us for that job, and the gov'nor bought up all the gear and had the sprit put aboard the *P.A.M.* The *Ella and Norman* didn't last long; she pretty soon sanded down."

We turned smartly up the Whitaker on the weather-going tide, then slacked off vangs and sheets and bore away through the Raysand. Presently the River Blackwater opened up with its fleet of laid-up ships—mostly crocks and casualties. The American *Helena Modjeska* was among them, for the two parts

had been towed there after she had broken her back on the Goodwins.

Our discharging berth lay behind Mersea Island on the far side of the Blackwater, but to reach it we had to run into Colne and up the Pyefleet Channel behind Mersea. George had never been up to the Strood, as the causeway connecting the island with the mainland is called. "The old man's been up plenty of times in the *Lancashire* and he says it's all right, but then he only draws about five foot and we're best part o' six. Tides are taking off, too. Get athwart some gutway and we've had it with all this stone aboard."

It was just seven o'clock when we came running into Colne. Brightlingsea lay to starboard with its usual cluster of yachts the smacks in the creek. But we were bringing up for the night in the mouth of the Pyefleet on the opposite side of the river.

I had been lazing in the sun on the hatch top. Presently I stretched myself and went forward with George to get sail off, stowing the staysail and brailing in the mainsail. Bill left the wheel to cast off the mainsheet, and the heavy canvas flogged wildly as I struggled with the lowers. We dropped the foresail, too, making it up by passing the clewline and hoisting clear of the windlass. Under topsail only *P.A.M.* reached in towards the East Mersea shore.

"She'll be all right here," said George, and let go the anchor.

* * * * *

We lay in Pyefleet all the next day while barges came in from sea. *Leofleda* had her staysail rigged as a spinnaker, with tack bowsed down by the mast case and the sheet led aft outside the rigging. Her skipper left the wheel and came to the rail.

"Where you for?" he shouted.

"Mersea Strood. Fetched up here last night from Upnor."

"Aye, aye. We come away from the Albert Dock yesterday morning and brought up last night just above the Whitaker Beacon."

Leofleda was bound for East Mills, Colchester, and was pushing on up Colne. She flew Marriage's colours—the *fleur-de-lis* on a blue flag, and had been in the wheat and flour

113

trade for most of her life. It was said her decks had never needed caulking in twenty years.

Other barges came in, too; the Colchester-owned *Ethel Ada,* and *Ethel Maud* belonging to Green Bros., of Maldon, with a large GB in her topsail—a survival from the old days whereby an owner might recognize his own barges coming in from sea.

Violet Sybil came in light, bound up for Alresford Creek to load sand; Goldsmith's *Scot* dropped down on the evening tide and brought up just above us.

We had visitors, too; the Customs officer called and stayed to tea. Later, a couple of fishermen pulled across from a nearby smack and passed a bucket of shrimps aboard.

"That's very good of you," said George. "How much?"

"That's all right, mate. We'd only be dumpin' em in the morning. They ain't no good to we." Then, as an afterthought: "What you got in?"

"Stone," George replied, and their faces fell.

"Pity about that fish," Bill remarked after they had gone. "They would have come in handy for supper."

"What fish?" we demanded.

"Why, didn't you see those flat fish in the sternsheets under a bit o' canvas? I see their tails sticking out."

George grinned. "They must've been disappointed us not having wheat or flour aboard. Nice lot o' shrimps for tea, though."

*   *   *   *   *

We mustered at 6.30 in the morning to find the breeze had died away to a flat calm and the motor boat from Wivenhoe securing alongside.

It was easy going at first up the Pyefleet, with plenty of water, but after three miles or so the channel narrowed and we grounded from time to time, so Bill and I went ahead in the boat to sound for the gutway. At last we were within sight of the Strood itself with withies dotted about here and there.

"They must be the ones George's old man stuck in," Bill declared. "He said to leave 'em close to port."

Even so, *P.A.M.* went aground again forty yards off the little wharf tucked away against the road, and a man sauntered down to meet us as we pulled ashore.

Apparently he was the foreman. "We've been looking for

114

you," he said. " It don't look as if you'll make it, not now
you've stuck out there, it don't. Owd tides are takin' off, too.
Don't start makin' fer another week, neither."

" That sounds lively," said Bill as we went back aboard, but
George refused to be dismayed. " I've met some of these old
gaffers before," he declared. " It's only just high water. We'll
make it all right."

The motor-boat opened up and we ran a line ashore. For
a few minutes *P.A.M.* remained fast, then slowly and almost
imperceptibly she started to move.

" Keep her goin'," George roared, beaming all over his face.
" Who said she won't do it? "

P.A.M. made it all right—but only just. The tide was done,
and we had to heave her right up into her berth. And all the
while the old chap stood watching with a baleful eye.

" That surprises me, that do indeed," he said, shaking his
head.

" Ah, but she's a special sort o' barge, this one! " George
declared. " D'you think they'll be starting on us to-day? "

" Not to-day, they won't, but I'll be phonin' in a few minutes
to let 'em know you're here, and I don't doubt but what they'll
be making a start good an' early in the morning."

The three of us went up the road at midday and found the
delightful old-fashioned *Peldon Rose Inn,* where a registered
letter was waiting for George, much to his surprise, with cash
in it.

" The gov'nor knows where to find us, anyway," said George.

" Must know it's a thirsty sort o' place," Bill added, with a
suggestive smack of his lips. " What's it going to be—bucket-
fuls? "

*　　*　　*　　*　　*

Before we had finished breakfast next morning eighteen
or twenty young Ukrainian displaced persons came down by
lorry and set about throwing out our stone. They were a cheerful, good-natured bunch only recently arrived from Italy.

At ten o'clock they took a breather. It was time, too, for me
to leave the *P.A.M.,* but Bill had laid out the cups on the
cabin top and brought up a great enamelled jug of tea.

" Better have a cuppa before you go," suggested George, then

beckoned to one of the gang who understood a few words of English.

"Tea! " he cried. "Come an' get it! "

The Ukrainian flashed a smile and bowed, then took off his leather gloves and called out in their own tongue to the others, who quickly gathered round.

Conversation was difficult, but they brought out their photographs and passed them for us to see. Then they pointed to various objects and wanted to know the English word for them.

"How you say? " they asked.

"Cup," Bill replied, then, turning to me, "Funny, ain't it, not knowing a simple thing like that? "

Sheila came up on deck and immediately became the centre of interest.

"How you say him? "

"Dog," said George firmly.

There was much head shaking.

"Him no dog! "

"Don't talk daft," said Bill, leaning over to scratch Sheila's ears. "You're our little dawg, ain't you? "

More gesticulations and more quick asides, then with a grin their spokesman exclaimed: "You milk him—huh? " Another vigorous shake of his head. "Him no dog! "

George and Bill slapped each other on the back and roared with laughter. With one accord they shouted, "You mean—bitch! "

They were still laughing and chattering when my Colchester bus came winding down the hill over on the Mersea side and across the Strood.

CHAPTER XI

TUBBY BLAKE—BARGE MASTER

"Capt. S. Blake,
"*Lancashire,*
"74, Bankside, S.E.

"Dear Mr. Bennett,

"Received your letter. Pleased to hear from you after all our trials and troubles. I note you have got over it with nothing but a few chips. I have been more fortunate. Of course I have been potted at numerous times, and the barge got well riddled, but I got missed—a little too big. I had forty-three bombs thrown at me at Ridge buoy one Sunday: quite exciting. They made a lot of holes in the water. Of course, we were an armed ship; we carried a Ross rifle and Hotchkiss and shield.

"Sorry the old *June* has gone west. Eastwoods have half a dozen old barges for sale at Otterham the same as mine, named after counties. That's where *Lancashire* came from. I note you have a house near the sea as a substitute, but I doubt if Mrs. Bennett will be satisfied with that. I had already heard you had a daughter.

"I towed down Thames on Monday and discharged on Tuesday, sailed on Wednesday and got to Whitaker Channel that Thursday. We arrived in Colne only to learn from George you had just left. We got back to Pitsea Holiday Monday, and we are loading stone here for the Colne.

"This is all. With best wishes, from

"Yours faithfully,

"S. BLAKE."

And now *Lancashire* was loading at Alresford, so the Brightlingsea Customs officer told us, and we were on our way upstream—George and I—in the hope of finding Tubby aboard.

"Mind you," said George. "He ain't the man he used to be. Time you knew him he weighed close on twenty stone, and now he's only fifteen." Then, as we opened up the Creek:

" There she is, Dad's little old *Lancashire,* up at the sand jetty just pulling out her tops'l. Proper yacht, she is! "

We rested on our oars while the light railway bridge spanning the creek slowly opened up and the deep-loaded barge came sailing through, shaking out her mainsail under way.

The topsail was white—or nearly so—like the patches in the mainsail where odd cloths had been renewed. The other sails, too, were no longer deep russet-red with oil and ochre dressing, but weather-washed and faded, with bare, yellowish chafes showing here and there in way of the brails. For all that, they seemed to fit her well enough.

Emblazoned on either bow was a freshly painted bright blue-and-white house flag standing out in startling contrast from the drab and dingy rail.

" Just look at her badges! " laughed George. " The mate must've been busy. Quarterboards done blue an' all! Dad don't hold with slapping on paint except he's on the yard—and that's not so very often neither. The last lot he brought away got adrift down the fo'c'sle, and you never saw such a mess. No, I reckon young John bought that drop o' blue out of his own pocket while the old man was away."

We pulled across to the *Lancashire.* The mate, a lean-faced, pleasant-looking youngster in glasses, was priming the pump with a bucket of water.

George pointed to the blue quarterboard. " Who's dead? " he demanded, for a blue band round a ship usually denotes a death in the firm.

" I am," flashed the mate, straightening up and sweeping the hair from his face. " Anyway, I shall be if I stay aboard this barge much longer."

George's father was standing by the wheel. Short and immensely thick-set, he swung slowly round, a monumental figure in shirt-sleeves, peaked cap and trousers that strove to constrain his massive girth, yet threatened to burst asunder at the slightest movement.

" That you, George? I didn't see you come up. 'Tain't your barge out there, I know."

" No, Dad. That's *Violet Sybil.* We're down river."

" What are you doin' up here, then? "

" I've brought someone you know to see you."

118

Tubby left the wheel and came to the side. "I thought I knew yer face," he exclaimed, after peering at me intently for a few moments. "'Ow are yer?"

Tubby stood with arms akimbo and bombarded us with questions while we made fast the boat.

"Waitin' to tow up Pyefleet? Never heard sich a thing! An' what's wrong with sailing up? I've bin up time an' agen. You don't want to worry about water. Jest let her blow up on the flood. You can't help but fetch up there all right."

"You'll be fetching up, too, if you don't watch out," George replied, heaving up the leeboard. "You're touching."

Tubby turned slowly to the wheel and bore up. "That's a fine thing," he declared, "settin' meself aground listenin' to all your claptrap," and his stomach began to shake as he chuckled to himself. *Violet Sybil* was towing past. He turned and stretched out a hand. "What's he want to go an' chuck away his freight on a tug for?"

George had obviously heard all this before. "It don't do to be too clever," he replied quietly, "specially if you're working to tides. This creek's all right with a fair breeze, but you've only got to so much as touch the bridge and you've had it."

But his father would have none of that. "Larst freight we brought away from Alresford, time we're loaded the wind's touchin' in. 'This ain't no good to us, John,' I says. 'Git up the stayfall an' we'll lower down.' So we did, too—*and* we poked her out through the bridge hole. Then we scrambled up the gear an' fetched away down Colne. That's right, ain't it, John?"

The *Lancashire* had sailed out her board. She came slowly up into the wind while the sails flapped lazily and the sprit lurched inboard. Tubby hove in on the mainsheet and deftly turned up on the kicking block. The foresail flogged for a while to and fro across the horse, then filled and was quiet.

Tubby gazed aloft reflectively. "Tawps'l sets pretty fair, don't it? That's not long since new, that ain't."

"And so's the mains'l—a good part of it, anyways," said George derisively.

His father chuckled again. "That's a good sail, that is. They tell me that one's twenty year old, not but what most of the cloths ain't bin renewed some time or other. This ol' barge

was in the brick work when the gov'nor bought her, an' used to have 'Eastwoods, Brickmakers' painted acrorst her sails in big white letters. You can jest about make out a C and a K if you look hard—they're the only two old cloths left, I reckon."

"What d'you expect?" said George. "It's a wonder you've got any canvas at all the way you cane her. I've seen you banging on up Swin when all the other barges put back many a time."

Tubby chuckled to himself. "I don't say but what we push her along. She's a smart little thing. You can sail on her, too. Times you's bloomin' well got to whether you like it or not. Same as larst Christmas Day, there come a breeze o' wind southerly an' we give it to her up So'west Reach fer to git home that night. First we blew the tawps'l out o' the ropes, and then the guts out o' the mains'l. Next the starb'd leeboard carries away, then the sheet pulls out o' the fores'l. Time we brought up we're right down under Sheppey.

"Then no sooner'n we got that little lot sorted out and a new tawps'l, we're comin' through Rays'n one day an' jest gybin' over when the spreet comes tumblin' down in halves. We had cargo in fer East Mersea, an' managed to fetch acrorst the Blackwater. Time we're empty the winds come away no'therly, so we ties a knot in the tawps'l and out we goes. I reckon she'd have looked up fer Maldon if we'd bin so minded. Yers, I do. Anyway, we let her blow into Bradwell an' gets on the phone to the gov'nor to send a new spreet down by road."

Tubby had been talking all the time, with his eyes fixed ahead. Now he made a ponderous trip to the lee guard rail, took a look round the foot of the mainsail and proceeded to put the barge about. She heeled gently to the evening breeze as she filled and paid off on the port tack. Water slopped on deck.

"Pretty deep, aren't you?" George remarked, and his father nodded.

"Ninety yards, that's all we've got in—sixty o' grit aft and thirty o' sand forrard. She sails better really with her head down a bit, but we've got to trim her by the starn on account o' that there clout we took on the starb'd bow roundin' up at New Hythe a few weeks back. They wanted us to go on the yard then. 'That's a fine thing,' I says. 'An' who's goin' to pay me,

25a Captain John Waterhouse — Pier Master at Strood.

b
Harold Margetts' racing crew.

John Waterhouse (seated) ;

C. Rich, Master of *Hibernia ;*

W. Bennett, Mate of *Harold Margetts;*

Charlie Woolmer, Master of *Caledonia.*

[*Sport and General*

7a Capt. Billy Austin,
n a more serious mood.

Will Everard, light
arge, close-hauled off
he Maplin Spit.

28*a*   Sea Reach, River Thames. *Mirosa* standing over towards the Kent shore, with the Mate pacing the weather deck.

b   *Ready* working up to Maldon in 1936. Since the war she has been renamed *Mirosa*.

29 The Swin would be a lonely, desolate waste without a barge or
two cracking on for the Spitway. *Leofleda* in all the sparkle
of a summer's morning, with the sands beyond, where seals
bask, and a coaster steaming up the Barrow Channel for
London River.

30a West Hoo Creek. The old *Bessie Hart*, winner of the Thames Barge Match i
1867, and *Partridge*. *Bessie Hart's* mast case still stands though her foredec
has long since gone.   b   "The Nore," Sea Wall. Elizabeth, Peter, Spanke
and friends.   There will be barges yet for Peter to sail.

31*a* Looking aloft on *June*, showing the topsail sheet leading down along the sprit.

b *Azima*'s brailed up mainsail, showing the lead of uppers and main brails. The sprit is supported by the mainsail headrope with the yard tackle half-way up to take the weight as she whips.

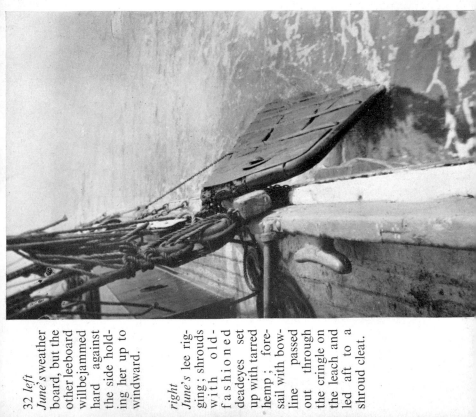

32 *left*
June's weather board, but the other leeboard will be jammed hard against the side holding her up to windward.

right
June's lee rigging; shrouds with old-fashioned deadeyes set up with tarred hemp; foresail with bowline passed out through the cringle on the leach and led aft to a shroud cleat.

time I'm on the yard? ' That wasn't no use to me, so off I goes ashore an' picks up a nice bit o' wood——"

"I like that! " said George scornfully. "Bit o' wood indeed! Orange box, more like! "

"As I was sayin', I gets some wood an' a bit o' felt an' heats up some tar——"

At that the mate who had been sitting quietly on the rail burst into a loud guffaw.

"Heat up some tar. Not half he didn't! He comes down the cabin with the tar pot and lights up the fire. Then he lays the wood and felt down on deck and slaps on the tar. Next thing he's kicked over the pot and got tar all over his boots. Time he gets forrard he's forgot the hammer and nails, so back he traipses right through the tar and down the cabin. There's so much tar about the deck he ends up by tarring all over."

"An' what's wrong with that? " Tubby demanded. "There's nothing to beat tarred decks. I always was handy with me tools, though. Not like some what's on the yard every five minutes."

He paused for a few moments before continuing. "Reckon we *shall* have to git seen to, though; we're makin' a tidy drop o' water now. She's never bin the same since we had wood pulp in fer Ridham that time. They started on us at eight in the mornin', and had it all out by nine. Only trouble was they had a go at the ke'lson an' tried to fetch that out, too! You know, this barge ain't never bin the same since. It's bin pump, pump all the time. That's right, ain't it, John? "

John nodded thoughtfully. "When I first come after a mate's job, the skipper says to me: ' Can you set a tawps'l? '

"'I dunno about that,' I says, an' nor I didn't.

"'Can you cook, then? '

"'Ain't much of a hand at cooking, neither.'

"'Can you splice an' tie a bowline? '

"'No,' I says, 'I can't.' Nor I couldn't, neither.

"'Well, let's see you try your hand at pumping,' so I pumps, and after I've been pumping for a while he says, 'That's all right. You're shipped! ' "

Tubby made no rejoinder, though his stomach shook with evident enjoyment. We were well down the Colne, almost to Brightlingsea where George's *P.A.M.* lay at anchor.

"Come alongside us for the night if you like, Dad," said George, but his father only shook his head. Just then George caught sight of the Pyefleet Buoy under our lee. "Watch out!" he shouted. "You're right on top of the buoy!"

"That's all right," said Tubby. "I know all about that," though it seemed impossible for him to see anything to leeward as he stood solidly at the wheel, never troubling to move or peer under the mainsail. Nor did he alter his voice, but just carried on in the same level, conversational tones, while the buoy slid by a couple of feet off the starboard quarter.

"I ain't bringin' up fer nobody," he declared.

"But you won't do any good pushing on to-night," George persisted.

Tubby left the wheel and turned on George with hand outstretched. "Now jest you listen 'ere. Say what you like, but I ain't bringing up in Colne an' that's flat! Who's goin' to sit up all night an' pump? Not you, I'll be bound. I ain't layin' here, and I'll tell you fer why. I'm carrying on into Rays'n and puttin' her ashore over on the Main fer the night. And d'you know what then? Why, we'll turn in, John an' me, an' git some sleep. Layin' on the mud'll do her a power o' good. That'll plug her, that will! And in the mornin' we'll git under way fust thing and be up at Pitsea to-morrow night."

Tubby never even glanced at us as we dropped into the boat and shoved off. Rumbling and chuckling, he leisurely put the *Lancashire* about, an unforgettable figure in shirt sleeves—individualist, a law unto himself, Tubby Blake—the complete barge master.

CHAPTER XII

"ON THE BUOY"

THE STORY OF AN OLD-TIMER

WE had towed down river astern of a string of lighters; our tug rounded up and was edging over towards the North Woolwich shore to put us on the buoys, when I caught sight of a gaunt, scruffy figure brandishing a paintbrush from the deck of a slab-sided coasting barge lying at anchor by herself with steeved-up bowsprit and high rails of a particularly drab shade of olive-green.

It was Sam, mate of the old *Pride*, and he was making violent signs for us to come alongside. The tug skipper had seen him, too, and turned with expectant, upraised hand.

Sam took our lines and we made fast. The *Pride's* decks were freshly painted a light blue-grey.

"It's a pity to mess 'em up, Sam."

"Don't you worry about that. The deck's bone dry an' the rail don't matter. No, I see you towin' down an' figured you'd have to bring up till next ebb. Fact is, I'm gettin' a bit tired out here all on me own."

"What's happened to the skipper?"

"The ol' chap, why, he's gorn home fer the week-end. We'd have bin on the buoy but fer me an' him havin' words. He don't mean nothin' really. You see, he'd gorn up to the city after a freight. The *Pride's* bin in the family fer years, and he likes to go around the brokers jest to see what's offerin'.

" 'I'll be perty late comin' off,' he says. 'You might keep the fire in so's I can git meself a bite o' supper.'

"After tea, though, Dick what's got the little ol' iron pot lyin' jest above us, he sings out, 'What about a run ashore, Sam?'

" 'Can't,' I says. 'Skipper's gorn ashore an' he'll be wantin' his supper time he comes off.'

" 'That's all right,' says Dick. 'Stoke up the fire. It won't hurt him to git his own supper fer once.'

123

" ' What about him comin' off? ' I says.

" ' That's easy. Jest leave yer boat on the hard. Reckon he'll find it if we should happen to miss him.'

" Well, that's what we done. Away we goes, an' what with one thing an' another, I must've bin a bit later comin' off than what I reckoned on, 'cos boat's gorn an' there's the ol' chap aboard dancin' around with the dip bucket.

" ' What's up? ' I says.

" ' Cabin bulkhead's alight.'

" So it was, too! Seems I'd stoked up the fire an' left the draft open at the bottom. Time the skipper's come off the cabin's full o' smoke an' soon as ever he shoves back the hatch the bulkhead catches. We got it out all right, but it made a rare ol' mess.

" Of course the ol' chap was upset. ' You've bin drinkin',' he says, ' an' nearly lost me me barge.'

" ' I ain't had but a couple of pints,' I says, which was true enough, for I hadn't got no more money, nor Dick neither.

" ' Better pack yer bag an' clear out,' he tells me, for the ol' chap was hoppin' mad.

" ' Don't take on so,' I says. ' I'll soon git the cabin tidied up.'

" Mind you, he never reckoned I'd go. He'd never bin able to git away home fer the week-end if I did. By an' by he simmers down an' that's how I come to be out here in the stream paintin' decks 'stead of layin' on the buoy. Said I'd have to stay aboard then."

Sam swung round and gazed at the decks with his head on one side. " Nice drop o' paint, that is."

I duly admired his handiwork, then turned to our own barge with her gear still lowered away on deck from the trip through the bridges.

Sam dropped his brush and leaped aboard. " I'll give you a hand to rig her," he said.

" What about your painting? You'd better have her looking smart for the old skipper when he comes off."

Sam made a grimace and wiped his hands on the seat of his trousers. " That's all right. I've done more'n he reckoned on. He don't know nothin' about the rail. That'll surprise him, that will."

124

"Yes," I agreed. "He'll certainly be surprised. The colour's a bit unusual, isn't it?"

Sam grinned. "It's all me own, in a manner o' speakin'. I scraped all round the tins in the forepeak. Queer ol' colour that makes. Well, come on, Let's git goin'."

We dogged the anchor and cleared the chain from the windlass barrel to make room for the stayfall, then shipped our handles. Sam spat on his hands and away we went.

There is a peculiar fascination in heaving up a barge's gear. The stayfall creeps round and round the stemhead block to the music of the windlass pawls, and all the while mast and sprit rise slowly and majestically from the jumble on deck. A pause for a breather and a quick look round, then down to it again with shortened handles. The tempo of the music quickens; shrouds and vangs and runners are coming taut . . .

"That's her," said Sam, straightening up and making to wipe the sweat off his face with his forearm. He stopped dead. "Lor' love us! Look what we've got here."

I swung round. Unnoticed by us, a lighter had come driving up on the young flood and was almost atop of us.

Sam clambered aboard the *Pride* and dashed aft to give her a sheer, but before he could release the wheel, there came a great crunching and grinding as the lighter reared up over our port rail. I tried to drop in a fender, but had to jump clear of the shovel-nosed swim.

For a while the lighter resisted our joint efforts to dislodge her, then as she fell alongside, so she came clear and began to drop aft. The lighterman remained silent all the while. Not so Sam!

"You silly young ——! You didn't ought to be allowed out on the river by yerself." Sam shook his head. His contempt for the modern young watermen was complete. "Better make a note of him, though I don't reckon he's done you no damage barrin' a bit o' paint. We always cop it a sight worse in the ol' *Pride* along of her rails standin' that much higher."

Sam took a seat on our quarter rail and searched in his pockets for the stub of a cigarette.

"Yers, high rails is all right at sea, but they're a bloomin' nuisance fer river work. Same as the docks now, we're always gettin' knocked about by lighters an' craft. Upsets the ol' chap

125

more'n anything I know of. He's a good ol' sort, even though he does sack me from time to time. Mustn't take no notice of what he says. That's jest his way o' goin' on like. I never see him raise his finger to nobody, an' I've bin mate along of him fer close on ten years—not till larst week, I didn't.

"That was funny an' no mistake. We were layin' on the buoy up at Greenwich along of a couple of Ipswich barges, an' me an' the ol' chap was on the foredeck splitting kindling wood, when we see a lighter drivin' up same as what that bloke done.

"'Better have a fender handy, Sam,' says the old 'un. 'Way the tide's a-settin' like as not we'll have her knockin' at our door.'

"Sure enough, she comes driftin' along atop of us, an' there's me flat on me belly tryin' to poke in a fender under her swim what's a-grindin' and splinterin' our rail somethin' cruel.

"'That's a fine thing to do,' says the ol' chap, shakin' his head sadly.

"But the lighterman, he was a foul-mouthed, flash sort with a powerful lot o' gold to his teeth. Started cursin' an' blindin'.

"That done it! Up jumps the ol' chap, roarin' like a bull. You'd never have thought a little 'un like him could have roared so loud. 'I'm comin' after you,' he shouts. 'Yers, I am.'

"Next moment he's nipped aboard the lighter, with a bit o' wood in one hand an' the chopper in the other. 'Jest let me catch you. I'll teach you manners, that I will!'

"All the chaps aboard the other barges come poppin' up on deck to see the fun. The lighterman starts squarin' up, so I grabs hold of the windlass handle an' starts after him.

"He never wanted no help from me, though. Not him! The sight of the ol' chap roarin' along the deck o' the lighter with a chopper was too much fer the lighterman. He drops his fists and takes to his heels.

"Laugh! You should've heard the cheering. 'Chop off his head,' one of the barge skippers shouts.

"'And so I will,' roars the old 'un, wavin' the chopper over his head. 'Jest let me lay me hands on him. I'll show him!'

"With that he puts on a spurt. The lighterman looks back over his shoulder proper scared. Jest then he trips over a bollard an' down he goes full length on deck. Up he jumps scream-

126

ing, with the ol' chap at his heels an' takes a flyin' leap down
the hold.

"I thought fer a moment the old 'un was goin' down after
him, but the lighter's got free by this time an' driftin' past, so
he takes a couple of swipes at the hatch coamin' an' nips back
aboard the *Pride* as fresh as a daisy.

"'Look here,' I says, 'you can't do that sort o' thing.'

"'Can't do what?'

"'Why, you can't go around chasin' people with a chopper.
You might have killed him.'

"'Oh,' says the ol' chap, 'you mustn't take no notice of
me. I never meant no harm, but somebody had to teach him
a lesson.'

"I reckon he did, too!"

CHAPTER XIII

A SAILORMAN GOES AFTER TIMBER

IT was just coming dark one day in August, 1947, when we turned into the Surrey Commercial Docks—George and I.

The policeman nodded cheerfully from the dimly lit doorway of his hut. "You're soon back," he said to George, skipper of the *P.A.M.* "What's the matter? Are they shut?"

George feigned indignation. "That's a fine thing. You must think we're a rough ol' lot in sailing barges."

The policeman rocked back on his heels, thumbs stuck in his belt, and chuckled. "I dunno about that, but you're usually a thirsty lot, you sailormen."

Sailing barges and bargemen are invariably dubbed sailormen in the docks. "Sounds nice and matey," George went on as we skirted a partially blitzed shed and picked our way gingerly past a sinister patch of oil. "But it's the sailormen that's always in the way, though."

The Greenland Dock was a study in light and shade. Work had stopped for the day, but clusters of lamps high up on ships' masts and upperworks flood-lit deck stacks of yellow timber and cast grotesque shadows over the dockside.

Our sailing barge lay alongside the Canadian s.s. *Harmac Westminster* tucked away in the shadows between her towering quarter and the quay. Bill, the mate, was working in the hold stowing timber that lay propped against the middle tie-beam—rough, unplaned boards, dumped down earlier in the evening. The skipper and I stripped off our coats and joined him.

"They were in a proper hurry this afternoon," said Bill, taking a breather. "I was on me own when they sung out to come alongside. 'We want you under our starb'd quarter,' they said, and it wasn't half a job, too, getting clear of all the craft. As soon as they'd slacked off the steamer's stern lines the cargo superintendent was all for heaving us in quick like. Only trouble was the topm'st got foul of her counter.

128

"'Hi!' I shouts, 'ease up.' But the big nob, all he thinks about is gettin' moored up again.

"'You're all right,' he says. 'Heave away, boys.'

"'Blow that fer a game,' I says to meself, so I ups an' tells him what to do with himself."

"And what did he say?"

"Told me to go an' do the same," Bill replied with a grin.

"That's all right," said George, "but when I get back aboard the cargo superintendent comes up to me an' says I'd better keep an eye on that young boy o' mine, and I didn't ought to let him swear off at people like that."

"Nothing to what you'd have said if the topm'st carried away," Bill retorted.

*   *   *   *   *

The docks came to life at eight o'clock next morning. Stevedores swarmed on board the ships and derricks swung into life. The cargo superintendent was soon about, a forceful personality in natty black pinstripe and a green pork-pie hat. He seemed to bear no grudge against the *P.A.M.* Twenty years' stevedoring and five years as a naval officer had hardened him off, so he said.

We had to shift to let a lighter in astern of us, so we hove ourselves ahead until our bows lay underneath the steamer's gangway. It was as near as we could get to the fourteen standards on the quay to complete our freight for Southend.

The skipper eyed the stack reflectively. "I don't reckon they'll get much of that in the fore hole," he said. "We'd better re-stow what we've got and shove the small stuff up forrard if we don't want to finish with an eight-foot stack."

The three of us turned to and half-emptied the main hold by sliding the longer lengths under the mast-case until the fore hold was full, then topping up in the hatchway with the short boards. The morning went. There was still no move to load us, and George went off to telephone the brokers. He came back with a long face.

"They reckon it 'ud cost fifty quid to put that lot aboard, what with loading charges and double handling, so we've got to go an' load five by twos from a steamer called the *Elkanah Crowell*. There's forty standards between us and the *Persevere*."

We went to the dock master's office and learnt that our

129

steamer was two days overdue, but that there was a ready berth waiting for her in the Albion Dock—the furthest of the Surrey Commercial Docks.

"That's a nice thing, that is," said George. "We'll get thirty bob for a shift. *And* we'll earn it, what's more! "

We had to wait until the lighters were loaded before the *Harmac Westminster's* stern lines were slackened off and we were able to warp ourselves out, inch by inch, stern first.

There were other sailormen in the dock. *Vicunia* and *Trilby* were both waiting for grain; *Leofleda* was lucky, for she went straight alongside the *Harmac Westminster* and loaded a full cargo of Canadian wheat in a few hours. *Primrose, Paglesham* and *Lorna* were after timber like ourselves.

The skipper went away in the boat to visit old Knocker in the *Lorna,* and took with him a young radio officer named Charlie from the American s.s. *Red Oak Victory,* who was greatly interested in sail and seemed to spend most of his spare time aboard us.

"They're terrible folk, them Yanks," Knocker declaimed, with a jerk of his thumb towards the flaring bows of the *Red Oak Victory.* "They went for my mate ashore larst night and made a proper mess of him. Rough ol' lot, they are. Bloomin' great knives an' buckets o' blood! That's their style."

Charlie remained silent until they came to go, when Knocker remarked to George, "I didn't know you had a new mate. Seems a nice quiet sort o' chap."

"Hear that, Charlie? Knocker thinks you'll do all right as mate."

"Can't stop now," Charlie drawled as he dropped into the boat. "I've got to get back aboard the *Red Oak* to sharpen up my knife and give the old bucket a bit of a clean-up for to-night! "

There was a light easterly air next morning for our trip round the docks. We hauled out the topsail sheet and hoisted sail, but halfway up the Greenland Dock, where lighters clustered about the ships on either hand, we met the great square-hulled coaling hoist *Wotan* in tow of a P.L.A. tug. And astern of us came a small motor tug with a string of craft.

"Down tawps'l," said the skipper, and we drifted in among the lighters, trying to make ourselves scarce.

"Where you for, Sailorman?" asked one of the lightermen.
"Albion Dock."

"You'll never make it by yerself, chum. Better take a tow. This chap coming up, he's going all the way."

While all the craft lay jammed tight, the mate jumped across and arranged matters with the motor tug. Slowly the *Wotan* drew clear and we emerged at the end of a string of empty barges and nosed up the cutting leading to the Canada Dock. As soon as the bridge opened there was a great surge of craft, but surprisingly little excitement, and our tugmaster, well versed in the art of dock-manœuvring, gradually forced a passage for his lengthy tow where none seemed possible.

The water here was littered with floating timber. In one spot there had formed a large accumulation of both new and oil-grimed deals past which a statuesque and bearded lighterman was poling his way with a boat hook. Halfway through, where the s.s. *Llandaff* lay on the buoys in the middle of the dock in addition to steamers lining the quays, passage was completely blocked by craft. Our tug only got through by setting the whole mass of timber-laden lighters on the move.

We cast off at the end of the Canada Dock into a reasonably quiet berth to await the arrival of our steamer. Right through the day lighters stacked high with timber drifted slowly down upon us. Sometimes tugs came to sort them out, and once a disgruntled lighterman with more craft to tend than he could manage, moaned bitterly when he arrived to find us hemming him in.

"You're finished, you b—— sailormen," he ranted. "If I had my way I'd blow the whole lot of 'em up!"

But Bill refused to be drawn. "Chuck us yer line, old 'un," he called, "and I'll give you a hand." A sailorman was always in the way. For all that, sailing barges have the right of free entry to the docks and do much of the transhipment work to the smaller outports.

It was late afternoon when the *Elkanah Crowell* steamed slowly up the dock into a solid phalanx of craft jammed tight round the *Llandaff*. A couple of hands on the fo'c'sle head dropped in fenders to take the worst of the bumps. Slowly but inexorably she forced a passage and shaped up for the cutting.

131

Following her came the *Wotan* again, and more lighters, and it was not until six o'clock when things had quietened down that we ran off a line and started to heave through.

The bridgeman greeted us with a stream of abuse. "And where d'you —— well think you're going? "

"Alongside our steamer that's just gone through," we replied.

"Come on, then. Get a —— move on." Then, just as we started heaving on the dolly winch, he changed his mind and yelled to us to lay off for a tug to come out.

We waited for a full twenty minutes. At last the bridge opened and the tug steamed through.

"Come on if you're coming."

George could stand no more. "I've just about had enough from you," he roared. "Just you shut yer mouth or I'll put in a report that'll shake you up."

"What he wants," Bill muttered, "is a good smack on the nose."

But the bridgeman had the last word. He was working late and hated the sight of us. As we hoisted the topsail he said with exaggerated sarcasm, "Ever read the back o' yer docket?"

"Drop yer sail! " George shouted, almost livid with rage.

"What for? " demanded the mate angrily. "You don't want to take no notice of him."

"Don't argue, Bill. Down tawps'l! "

The bridgeman locked his hut and made off, leaving George fuming, for the craft docking note or docket forbids any vessel to sail within the docks. "All the same, barges are always sailing in the docks," George muttered to me, "and nobody says anything about it. Why, I've seen my old dad turn up through the docks before now with a couple of fenders hanging over his bows to bounce him off the docksides coming about."

It was quiet in the Albion Dock. Work was finished for the day. We hoisted the topsail again, but the breeze died on us and we had to work our way as best we could round the steamers on the buoys and alongside the *Elkanah Crowell* over on the far side. Our parcel, so her second mate told us, was some way down the forward stack. Apparently she was late because her bunkers caught fire on the trip across from Finland, and she had to put into Stockholm with a list of thirty-five degrees.

Work started in the morning. The deck stack chains were cast off, and a couple of gangs of stevedores went to work quietly and methodically to the accompaniment of the winches. All round the dock echoed that peculiarly attractive sound of timber; timber dropping into craft; timber being stowed and stacked. It was timber everywhere; sweet-smelling stuff gleaming·bright in the sunshine.

The men made up their own sets on board with one end chocked up to allow the sling to pass beneath. The winchmen and winches followed the barely perceptible movement of the foremen's fingers as if by telepathy. The tally clerks stood chatting to each other as they leaned over the rail with only a cursory glance as the derricks swung out.

" Of course we count 'em. How many d'you make in that set? . . . Thirty-six? Sixty-two, more like! Eight fours, six threes, five twos an' a couple o' singles. Easy, see? " Then pulling his tally sheet from its protecting sheath of newspaper and making an entry: " As I was saying . . ."

Down in the lighter they erected a thwartship beam for each set to drop on as it came overside. Once a fresh set landed on top of another and sent the timber flying. The stevedores scattered but never said a word, while the foreman looked up quickly at the winchman, who galvanized into life and spoke for the first time that morning. " You moved yer fingers," he insisted. " Yers, you did. You moved yer fingers."

There was far more excitement when the sling accidentally knocked over a set that had just been made up, and a wizened little old chap in a blue silk shirt leaped to protest bitterly. Yet there was nothing involved beyond merely building up the set again.

We watched the deck stack slowly diminish and calculated our chances for the morrow. They thought they might be starting on our parcel Friday afternoon, but shortage of craft held up the work. The stevedores who had started the day on piece work now automatically reverted to day work, and came after a pack of cards to while away the time.

It was late afternoon before they were able to start again. A lighter arrived, and a group of stevedores jumped aboard to swing her. One little chap with a protruding tooth was holding on a line to the *Elkanah Crowell*.

"Heave up, Jim," they shouted from on board.

"I've got her," Jim replied with a confident grin. "Don't you worry, I've got her."

But when the strain came Jim was left with the bare end and no place on which to make fast. He looked over his shoulder in desperation, while the rest of the gang yelled encouragement. Either he let go or went overside. Then came the final exhortation: "Take a turn round yer tooth, Jim!" But to everybody's disappointment Jim let go.

Saturday morning came. The motor-barge *Persevere* arrived. She, too, was after five by twos. Her skipper took a quick look at the stack and went off home for the week-end. By a quarter to twelve all work had stopped, and within a few minutes the docks were deserted. The sun shone and an ethereal hush settled everywhere. Only an occasional lighter piled high with timber drifted slowly past to fetch up of her own accord at the leeward end of the dock.

The mosquitoes alone showed signs of life. It was time for me to pack my bag.

*   *   *   *   *

P.A.M. got her parcel Monday afternoon, making twenty-six standards in all, so George told me later, and sailed out through Canada Dock again that night with a four-foot stack on deck. They locked out into Limehouse Reach at daybreak.

"That's right," he said. "We locked out first thing and picked up a smart breeze westerly. We were down on Southend the next morning.

"'We've been looking for you for the past week,' they told me. 'Where have you been hanging about all this time?'"

CHAPTER XIV

A LIFETIME OF BARGING

DURING the summer of 1948 I sometimes stepped off the train at Strood for a chat with old John Waterhouse, who taught me to sail *June* years before the war. He had been in barges all his life, and had no regrets.

" It's a good life," he said. " Plenty o' work, a good barge, and decent owners, and there's nothing to touch it." He had seen barges in their heyday and raced against the best of them. His life-story was really the story of barges.

" You know, Skipper," I said to him one quiet evening as we sat on a bench by Strood Pier, " it's a pity you can't get some of it down on paper."

" What, me? " he laughed. " No, no, I couldn't do that."

" Suppose I wrote it for you? " I suggested. " Would you mind that? "

John sat still for a moment, then turned towards me and lay his arm along the back of the bench. "All right," he said. " Let me see now. Where do we start? . . ."

*   *   *   *   *

John Waterhouse was born at Upper Upnor on the River Medway in 1862, and went to sea with his father at the age of thirteen as cabin boy in the barge *William Little*.

" She was a 120-ton swimmy barge, tops'l rigged, with a handspike windlass. I was only a little nipper at the time, an' they had a special little bar made for me. ' Steady now,' my ol' dad used to say when I jumped up on the barrel an' tried to heave up on me own. ' Steady now, not too quick! '

" We used to load loam for the foundries up at Blackfriars and the Hole-in-the-Wall. An' we took a tidy lot o' clay away from Upnor time they were workin' on the London Docks. They loaded us at the clay stage agin the woods, with women an' boys workin' along o' the men. It was out along the stage, then up barrow, an' tip right into the barge. Tidy weight, them barrows, too! "

135

John sailed in several of the barges belonging to the Little family. As mate of the *Charlotte Little,* he worked up the Regent's Canal to Paddington.

"We had to unship our leeboards before going up the Cut, then when it come to the tunnel, we had to lay on our backs an' work our way through with our feet agin the roof. Captain Cogger was a fat ol' chap. 'Now look here, you young b——,' he said, 'don't you go shovin' too hard, or we'll git stuck.' An' so we did, too!"

After a short spell with his uncle in the 220-ton barge *William and Elizabeth Little,* young John went master of the *Isabella Little* at the age of nineteen.

"I stayed in her for close on nine year—chance work mostly with a freight o' casked cement now'n agen. Then we come round to the Medway with breeze from Poplar Commercial Gas Works for the West Kent, an' dropped down to Clinkham after a freight o' chalk. There was a rare lot of Essexmen waiting on turn, so we lay off to our anchor an' went home. That night it come on to blow a gale o' wind. Next thing there's a telegram from the mate of the *Florence Little*: 'Come at once; barge sunk.'

"That was a nice ol' how d'you do! Seems she'd driven up over her anchor an' holed herself. I go chasin' up, but couldn't do no good, and I had to send word back to the gov'nor.

"Up he comes and has a look at her. 'We'll have one more go,' he says, but she'd got too big a hole and we couldn't quite manage it, though we brought off men with pumps from shore. In the end we had to fetch Mr. Curel, the barge builder, from Strood, and he patched her up and got her down on the yard.

"Funny thing was that freight o' chalk was going to be my last in the *Isabella,* for Curel's had just about finished building the *Daisy Little,* and I was to have her. Imagine how I felt when the gov'nor says to Mr. Curel, 'What d'you think of him? Sinks one barge and then comes along for another!'"

Daisy Little was a 120-ton barge with 5-ft. 11-in. sides and a fine bold sheer. She was launched on the last Saturday before Christmas, 1890, and cost £950. "Curel was a good barge builder, but what you might call a bad friend to himself. He used to have to wait for his money and sometimes fell down.

Not that we didn't pay up, for I remember taking the last fifty quid along meself an' gettin' the receipt."

She was built with an eye to racing—" Specially lined off for it "—and it so happened, with their steam hoy laid up with boiler trouble, Gamman's were looking for a smart barge to run between Chatham and South Devon Wharf, just below Tower Bridge.

"Mr. Gamman, he says to me, 'Can you do two freights a week?'

"'If you can guarantee me a breeze I'll do it,' I says. He just laughs and tells me to do me best and he'll make it all right with me afterwards. Well, we had six months of it, and twice we got beat by the tide in Chatham Reach, an' they sent down men to track us up along the wall, so's we shot acrorst the water an' got unloaded the same day.

"When we'd finished up, the ol' gentleman come and tapped me on the shoulder. 'You've done all right,' he says, and give me five quid."

Daisy Little was entered for the 1891 Thames Barge Match in the Topsail Class, and had the bad luck to carry away her jib outhaul after leading round the Nore. She came in second to Goldsmith's *Pastime,* sailed by the redoubtable Harry Munns.

But in the Medway match John Waterhouse turned the tables and won a great race by half a bowsprit.

"Harry Munns come up to me afterwards. He was a stern sort o' chap. 'Boy, you done very well to-day.' I had to smile, and he didn't like that. 'There's nothing to laugh at!' he said.

"I reckon there was, though, for he wanted a tidy bit o' beating, and comin' out o' Sheerness that time, with us creepin' up on his weather, he makes to shake her up till all me crew start a-hollerin', 'Look out! She's winding!'

"I was lookin' out all right. Sailing hard same as we were, I couldn't see the wheel, but I did catch a glimpse o' the tip of his rudder. He wasn't windin' at all, but bearing away in spite of his capers, so I jest held on an' drew clear."

John Waterhouse made some remarkable passages in the *Daisy Little.* He came away from Rotherhithe at 6.30 one morning bound for Margate with coal. They hung on to their spinnaker all the way, and presently the mate called to John

137
K

to come forward. "She was piling up such a bow wave the water come spurtin' up through the hawse-hole jest like a fountain. I stood an' watched, it was that pretty." They were in Margate by 3.30 the same afternoon.

Coals to Margate paid 2/- per ton, of which the owner took one-half and the other half was divided between skipper and mate in the traditional proportion of two to one.

On another occasion the *Daisy Little* lay at anchor off Upnor when they got orders to sail for Beckton to load coke.

"We got away from Upnor at half-past six in the morning an' carried a smart no'therly breeze round to the Thames. There was some weight in it, too, I can tell you! We were round off Beckton jest as the men were knockin' off for dinner.

"'What you after, Cap'n?' sings out the wharf manager.

"'Coke,' I says.

"'Come on, then. I'll get the men back to see to you afore dinner.'

"They had us loaded an' away inside the hour. We come away down with coke on deck two hatches high, and made another re'ch of it all the way, so's we're brought up off Upnor agen by seven o'clock tha' same evening. They couldn't credit it ashore we'd bin away up to Beckton till they see we're coke-loaded."

In 1893 the *Daisy Little* was again entered for the Thames Barge Match, and went up on the yard at Greenhithe, where she was rigged out with a bowsprit.

"Blackleaded her sides? I looked after that, don't forget! We sandpapered her bottom, what's more! "

The tides were very poor the day before the race, and *Daisy Little* got neaped on the blocks. The only way to get her off in time was to jack her up, then knock away the upper blocks and lower her down. "That was a night, that was! There wasn't hardly any water in the river. We only jest got her off even then, but Keep's *Baltic* at Northfleet never flet at all. She got be-nipped on the blocks and missed the race."

The course was from Gravesend to the Nore and back to Erith. The crew of the *Baltic* shifted into another of Keep's barges, the *Pacific,* and sailed as an unofficial entry for the sheer joy of it. It was a wild day, with a strong south-westerly

breeze. *Wm. Paxton* and *Britannia* lost their topmasts, but *Daisy Little* carried all her canvas on the long beat up river, though she had two deck seams under water most of the time.

"The most wonderful feat of the whole business was this," reported the *Sportsman*. "The *Daisy Little*, before they entered Gravesend Reach, had weathered the whole fleet, but off Rosherville a heavy puff caught her and she was nearly on her beam ends as possible, and there were fearful shouts that she had gone over, but she righted herself luckily in time. . . ."

"That's right," said John Waterhouse. "There was some hollering all right. Our anchor chain was on deck flaked down on the headledge. Time we dabbed down with water halfway up our coamings, blowed if she didn't shoot the lot overboard. Funny thing was nobody saw it go but us.

"We dragged it across to Gibbs's while we bent on the ol' chopper block we always kept in the mastcase, to buoy it with. 'Stand by,' I shouted, 'and knock out the shackle pin when I sing out.' Then I come about an' stood acrorst till White's yard lined up with the ol' ballast engine called the *Diver*, and let it all go.

"Keep's *Pacific* was out ahead of us, but he stood on too fer into Greenhithe. We made a short dodge and fetched out ahead of him an' beat the lot on 'em—first-class barges an' all! By rights we'd have brought up at Erith along o' the others, but I didn't want to let on we'd shot our chain, so I sings out we're slipping down right away as we'd bin promised for committee boat in the Gravesend regatta next day.

"'But what about yer flag?'

"'Can't wait,' I says, knowing full well the crew'd have a job to keep from talkin' with a few drinks inside 'em. Besides, we'd plenty o' good food aboard, so we'd not go short even though we did miss the supper ashore that night. And that's what we done. We dropped down till I picked up me bearings, then Mr. Goldsmith, who'd had the *Tricolor* and *Pastime* in the race, blowed if he didn't come sailing past in his yacht.

"'Congratulations!' he sung out.

"'Thank you, sir,' I shouts back, then says quietly to the crew: 'Now look here, don't go on hollerin' an' bawlin' about. Come aft an' whisper when you spot the chopper block and I'll put her up on it as close as I can.'

139

"They hooked it with a hitcher an' got a couple o' turns round the windlass in double quick time an' scrambled it aboard. You never saw anything like it in yer life; all burnished bright as silver, it was, from draggin' over the bottom. Time we're down off Gravesend we're all shackled on an' shipshape with nobody the wiser."

Daisy Little worked along the Kent coast as far as Broadstairs with coal, coke, chalk, ballast, sand and the like.

"We come out o' Margate one afternoon and lay up along the coast past Herne Bay. It had been looking a bit curious out to the west'ard and soon it come on to blow good an' hard. Wasn't long afore we had our tops'l goin' all to pieces. Wind was touchin' on, and there were bloomin' great strips o' canvas a-sailin' in over Herne Bay. We went in under Shell Ness that night, then up into Sheerness and on to Greenhithe.

"Next morning Henry Little comes down to the wharf like he usually did most mornings soon after nine.

"'How are we getting on, John?' he says, all bright an' cheery.

"'All right,' I says. 'Blown out the tops'l, though.'

"'Oh,' he says. 'I'll have to send the sailmaker down to stitch it up.'

"'Stitch it up, Gov'nor! Why, I reckon he'd want a tidy lot o' thread with stitches all the way to Herne Bay an' back!'"

But there was no topsail forthcoming, and John struck his topmast and sailed for a year stumpy fashion. "She got along pretty fair an' all!"

In 1897 John left the *Daisy Little* and took the *Lilian* belonging to A. R. & S. Sales, Ltd., of Woolwich, staying in her for twelve months, mostly engaged on Government stores and magazine work. Then came a vacancy with the West Kent Cement Company, which John had been looking for, and he went master of the 115-ton *Arthur Margetts*, trading with cement from the Medway to the various London docks and depots at 1/6 per ton, and loading back with small coal and coke.

"All the West Kent barges had varnished spars and flew a red bob with a white star. Had a star, too, in our tops'ls so's they could pick us out comin' up river, for there was a tidy few barges tradin' up above Rochester in those days.

"I stayed in the *Arthur Margetts* seven years and four months an' never had much trouble, though once we lay at Rotherhithe and a tug comin' up got put by for a steamer an' come in athwart our stem and damaged it. But I was pretty lucky—always have been!"

In 1906 John took the *Harold Margetts,* a slightly larger barge of about 120 tons; 77-ft. by 18-ft. 6-in., with 5-ft. 11-in. sides. She was built by Curel at the Lower Yard, Frindsbury, in 1890. "She was what you'd call a nice comfortable barge, and you could always lay down an' go to sleep, with no pumpin' nor nothin' o' that sort. They were all good barges in the West Kent, and we used to look after them same as if they were our own."

Barges bound up river for the same wharf raced each other for turn as far as Chatham Point. "We had a strong wind comin' up once, with our *Hibernia* and a barge named *Shannon* astarn of us. We git into Chatham Reach an' the fore shroud breaks. Soon as that went, the other two went an' we blowed the whole lot out on her!"

Coming up Limehouse Reach was the time for preparing to lower away the gear; anchor chain was thrown off the windlass, and three turns of the stayfall taken round the barrel. Then, with the strain taken, the stayfall stopper was cast off and the tack of the foresail let go.

The huffler would come aboard in Bridge Reach to give a hand. "Crosswell was our man. Used to pay him five bob. He'd take the wheel, seein' as he knew all about the set o' the tides, and I'd lower away while the mate sees to the sails. Same as turning up through, we'd keep everything on her right up to the bridge—had to at nips an' precious little run in the tide —then down tops'l an' shoot her up through. Mind you, you had to be pretty smart lowerin' down, with no ridin' turns nor nothin' o' that sort.

"Soon as you're lowered down, you've got to tie up the end o' the stayfall with a little bit o' line an' heave up as smart as you like so's to git her under way agen.

"Sales's barge *Gertie* come up one day. Her stopper wasn't off when they come to lower away an' got the whole lot knocked out of her. Another time, one o' Jimmy Little's barges, he come

141

up through an' was jest heavin' up when the stayfall breaks and the skipper gits killed.

"I've gorn up through the middle once and blowed back through the Strood arch. Enough to break yer heart, that is! Had to rig her an' go through next day. Couldn't do no more that tide.

"I remember going through the bridge another time, and when we got through the tops'l got full o' wind and broke off the topm'st like a carrot.

"My ol' huffler looks at me. 'That's a nice thing,' he says. 'An' what do we do now?'

"'Do?' I says. 'Why, I reckon we'd better put the kettle on an' have a cup o' tea!'"

The West Kent works were taken over by the Associated Portland Cement Manufacturers in 1912, and their barges became merged in the "Blue Circle" fleet.

In 1927 *Harold Margetts* was entered for the newly revived Thames and Medway Barge Matches, and was hove up on the covered slip at the Upnor barge yard of the A.P.C.M. for a month. She was fitted out with a bowsprit and all new gear. "They never done her bottom like the *Daisy Little*." Nevertheless she won first prize in the river class in the Thames race. "Then we come round and dead-heated with the *Plinlimmon* in the Medway. They never bargained for that, and when we went up for the prizes, Mr. Willis, the Commodore, he fished out half-a-crown from his pocket.

"'Here you are,' he says. 'You'd better toss with the other captain.'

"But Scott didn't want to toss. He thought he'd won in the *Plinlimmon,* and I don't doubt but what it seemed so to him with a shorter bowsprit, so I says: 'It's all right, Gov'nor. Both the barges are in the same firm. I won in the Thames, so it's only right an' fair to give it to him.'

"Mr. Gill, though, who ran the Medway match, he wouldn't have it. 'That's very sporty of you, Waterhouse,' he says, 'but we'll share out the money and get another flag made special.'"

In 1929 the A.P.C.M. staged their own barge match, starting from anchor off Upnor and sailing round the Nore and back.

"We had a strong wind down, but it fell away light comin' back, and time we're at the top o' Saltpan Reach I goes away

on me own to the west'ard to look for a breeze. Blowed if it
don't come southerly and away they go—the rest on 'em—
with us becalmed. Still, we come in second, one minute after
Plinlimmon."

In 1930 *Harold Margetts* raced again in the staysail class,
taking second prize in the Medway match and fourth prize in
the Thames match the following year.

John Waterhouse retired in 1932 at the age of seventy.

But even then his sailing days were not yet done. He came
away with us in *June* and showed us how to handle a barge.
Then the A.P.C.M., too, brought him back to sail the *Harold
Margetts* against their *Marconi,* which they had fitted out for
the barge match.

"We were that fer ahead going down river, but when we got
back into Sheerness the wind come down sou-west. We were
turnin' to wind'ard, and there was him comin' along astarn
with the wind easterly. Dammed if we didn't do him, though,
and *Marconi* was a proper racing barge!"

*　　*　　*　　*　　*

Daisy Little later went to work for the Gillingham Portland
Cement Company and sported a white bulldog in her topsail.
Now she is fitted out with a derrick as a wrecking barge, and
lies off the " Ship and Lobster " at Gravesend.

Pacific has been running as a motor-barge for Whiting Bros.
until July, 1948, when she blew ashore at Whitstable one
blustery night.

Arthur Margetts fell on bad times, and was in the Thames
ballast and rough stuff work before the war.

Plinlimmon was converted to a yacht. So, too, was *Marconi,*
which sank while serving as naval accommodation vessel in
Ramsgate inner harbour, and lay there for the rest of the war
with her wheelhouse just awash, festooned with weed.

Harold Margetts was on powder work during the war and
finished up in Oare Creek, looking very bedraggled, but she
has taken on a new lease of life, converted to a smart yacht
barge.

Most of the other old-timers are gone. But old John Waterhouse himself is still going strong at the age of eighty-seven.
He is pier master now at Strood.

CHAPTER XV

MALDON'S *MIROSA*

IT was a sparkling morning in June, 1948, when I went to Maldon to look up Billy Austin.

Mirosa lay at the Hythe Quay, a typical, beamy, shallow-sided Maldon barge, built by Howard in 1892. She looked well in the morning sunlight, fresh from Cook's yard; the sails had just been bent after a dressing of fish-oil and ochre, and her skipper, Billy Austin, was padding about the deck, shackling on the foresail sheet and chatting the while with a group of early risers on the quay.

"May I come aboard, Skipper? "

Billy looked up at me and smiled. It was high water, and the barge had blown out a foot or two. "Yes, yes," he said. "Come aboard if you can git."

I dumped my bag on the cabin top, and the mate invited me down below, where there was a pot of tea on the table, but hearing the water bailiff come alongside in his motor-boat, he left his own cup and dashed up on deck. A barge can turn away down from the Hythe Quay, but a friendly tow saves a lot of hard work at times.

"Mind you, he doesn't do it for everyone," said Billy, when I joined him on deck a little later, but I remembered getting a similar tow in *June* before the war, and laughed, whereupon Billy's face wrinkled into a grin and he nodded towards forward. "You can give Jack a hand with the tawps'l if you like."

We hauled out the sheet and hoisted away. It was a big sail, and I was amazed how easily we set it; *Mirosa* was obviously well found with blocks and running gear.

"She'll fetch now," said Billy quietly, so we cast off the tow line and gave her the foresail. Then he pointed to the mainsail and began to overhaul the sheet.

"Shall I let her run? " asked the mate, with his finger on the pawl.

Billy nodded, and the heavy folds of the still wet mainsail

144

MALDON'S "MIROSA"

fell out. He quickly trimmed the sheet and made fast on the spiked block that clattered over the wooden horse. "That's a big owd block, that is. You want to watch yourself with him."

We were clear of Maldon now, with its line of smacks moored head and stern along the broad sweep of the shingle beach, and the ebb was already beginning to creep down as we bore away round Herring Point.

Billy swung round and looked back at the little town on the hill. "Yes, yes, we had to go up on the yard to have our stem seen to. A whole lot o' lighters come athwart us up at Woolwich. You know how it is at the Docks. One of 'em ties up at the knuckle and a dozen or more hang on. Comes a puff o' wind and they're all adrift, driving up on the flood. Proper owd job, that was. Meant new apron, too—— All right, Jack. We'll let her gybe! "

Billy and his mate had been together for many years, first in *Mermaid,* which Billy had had for twenty-eight years, then for fourteen years in his present barge, *Ready,* as she was named until a year or so ago when Trinity House were particularly anxious to use the name for their new lightship tender, hence the newly christened *Mirosa.*

The skipper stooped to drop the leeboard. "You'll have to excuse the muddle down below. We haven't had a chance to git straight. Even had to put the clean bedding down the hold. I was reckoning on a day or two to give the decks a lick o' paint and git cleared up below before we went away, but the gov'nor was round Maldon yesterday having a dig at us. Said there were only two of our barges up in London, so I said we'd git away up."

He walked over to starboard and clung to the boat davit while he looked out ahead. We were on a reach now: I made to heave up the weather board, but he shook his head. "Leave her be," he said. "That helps her sail, that does. She's jist balanced now as she is. Heave up the board and she'll carry weather helm."

Billy Austin is something of a legendary figure in these waters. His always were the best cut sails; his gear beyond reproach. Vang fall blocks were of wood—outside blocks—and infinitely kinder than the ubiquitous metal variety.

I remarked on the unusually wide decks, and Billy's eyes

145

twinkled. "Jist the thing for stack work," he said, "but that
takes a powerful lot o' shovelling when you're trimming grain."
His face wrinkled in mock disgust. "They poured it into us in
an hour once. No, this owd barge was built for the stack work
time there was plenty of hay for London River. Funny thing,
though, we'd have loaded straw up at Colchester this trip but
for Horlock's *Redoubtable* being due up there and promised
a freight by the gov'nor." He stooped and eased off the mainsheet. "Happen there'll be plenty o' wind up Swin. We'll have
a good owd sail, though I doubt we'll carry our tawps'l all
day."

We came sweeping down past the last of the fleet of war
relics moored in the Blackwater; *Samlong,* with an engineroom
full of water and a light lashed to the muzzle of her gun aft;
another Liberty ship with a great gash in her starboard quarter,
and the old liner *Cairo City*. The crocks are gradually dis-
appearing. Even the *Helena Modjeska* has gone to the breakers.
But West Mersea was full of craft, with yachts and smacks
and oyster dredgers in hundreds. It seemed incredible that
barges ever worked up to the Hard.

Billy grinned. "We used to go up at night! That's right.
Hung out our navigation lights and sailed up through. Wasn't
our fault, same as we picked up a boat or two that wasn't
showing a light! "

Bradwell, over on the south side of the Blackwater, is
another little port whose sea trade has gone. There were plenty
of yacht masts beyond Peewit Island, but never a barge's sprit.
The half-tide, sunken quay remains with its eerie collection of
totem-like poles to fend off craft at high water, but Bradwell
was finished as a port when London's horse buses disappeared.

Billy remembers Bradwell in its heyday. There was plenty
of life in these parts once upon a time.

"Over there on St. Peter's Point, back o' Brad'll, where
they've built the aerodrome, that's where we used to git ashore
after hares. Many's the time I've bin crawling out one side
of a ditch, with the keeper crawling down the other. Rare owd
goings on, there were, with fake whiskers an' all! "

"As for the chapel on the Point, why, I recall when it was
jist a ruin, knee-deep in cow dung. Proper wild part, that is,
and nobody there but for one owd chap in a little bit of a

cottage. He used to live all on his own, wildfowling and fishing, though whether he's still there I don't jist know."

We luffed up for the Raysand Channel, with the low sea wall of the Main stretching away to the southward as far as I could see. It was here, in little creeks known as outfalls, barges used to load hay and sailed for London River with great stacks on deck halfway up the mainmast and the mate perched on top to keep a lookout. And when they fetched up in the Pool, they had to set to and clear away trusses from amidships so as to lower the gear and dredge up through the bridges.

There was another barge away over the Spitway—six miles off, at least—which Billy declared was the *Will Everard*. I remembered then having seen her at Colchester discharging Yorkshire gas coal, and she must have come out from Colne on the morning tide.

"She'll be bound up light for Greenhithe," said Billy. "Spitway is no use to us though, not bound up Thames with the wind westerly. Better be half lay up through Rays'n and make a fair wind of it out to the Whitaker. Besides, there's precious little water in the Spitway these days. Some of our chaps bound for Ipswich grounded there the other day and paddled around. Mind you, that was low water springs, but they never found but nine inches. That's sanded up badly, that has."

All this time the mate had been busy in the fo'c'sle, clearing out and stowing gear. Now he came aft and lit a cigarette.

"Kettle on?" asked Billy.

Jack nodded and went below. There came sounds of the fire being poked into life, and the rattle of mugs on the table.

The skipper turned a wrinkled face to me, for a smile seemed to hover perpetually about those brown eyes. "We don't bother much about a meal under way, but a cup o' tea, now that always goes down well."

It was not too healthy out here by the Whitaker during the war. Goldsmith's *Ailsa* was mined out beyond the Beacon. Others were shot up. And there was always the wreck of the old *Florence Myall* on the Ridge. "That wasn't so bad while the mast was in her, but that's gorn now. Take the bottom out of a barge on a dark night, that owd wreck would." A smile flitted across Billy's face. "Same as the first war, when

147

the patrol boat caught us airing down along the edge of the Maplins one night.

"'What barge?' he sings out.

"'*Mermaid*,' I says.

"'You know very well you're not allowed to sail in a defended area after dark.'

"'That's right enough, but nobody's going to take us for a Jerry. Besides, they want us round Maldon in a hurry.'

"He began to blow off at that. 'That's no matter. Jist you drop your hook, else there'll be trouble.'

"Well, we had our anchor on deck, but the patrol boat couldn't see that in the dark. 'All right,' I says to the mate quietly. 'Leave the anchor be, but make a good owd noise chucking chain over the windlass barrel.'

"So we dropped our fores'l and rounded up. Then I sung out to let go, and the officer must've thought we'd anchored, but as soon as the M.L. was gorn, away we went over the Ridge and acrorst the Main. I knew it wasn't any use trying to git into the river by night, so we made for the smacks over on the North Buxey. No sooner we'd dropped anchor, though, we're hailed again.

"'What ship?'

"'*Mermaid*.'

"That did it! It was the same chap as before. Swear! Dear, oh, dear! I've never heard the like o' that before nor since."

Luffing up close-hauled inside the Beacon, we came up with the *Will Everard*, light barge, steel built, the biggest on the coast. She came ramping in towards us on the opposite tack, but sagged away on the ebb, and eventually winded four or five cables astern.

We had our tea, sweet, piping hot stuff with tinned milk; the finest tea never tastes half as well ashore! Then the skipper took a long look at the *Will Everard* and got down to the serious business of sailing his barge to windward. Jack started work on the mahogany panelled cabin, clearing out the lockers and sorting over the junk, but every time we came about as we worked the shoal water along the edge of the sands, he came tumbling up on deck, paused for a moment as if to get his bearings, then shuffled away forward to tend the foresail.

Mirosa had a lovely suit of sails, cut to perfection, and at

148

the topmast truck flew out stiff and straight a brand new gold and purple bob, the handsomest of all the barge house flags. With a smart sailing breeze and a clean bottom, this looked to be *Mirosa's* day indeed. Billy chuckled quietly to himself, his brown eyes agleam, when suddenly he caught sight of the *Will Everard* on the same tack as ourselves, but out on our weather quarter and holding right up into the land.

"Well, well, jist you look at that! The *Will's* picked up a no'therly slant."

She had it all to herself, carrying it with her on a long board that brought her chasing up, while we turned away to windward and only just managed to head her at the Maplin Spit Buoy.

"We start even now," was Billy's only comment. The free puff had gone. If anything, the breeze was a little south of west. "More likely to souther out, I reckon."

There was a whole fleet of loaded barges running down S.W. Reach. First came Paul's *Jock* under power, stumpy-rigged at the time, with white mainsail and foresail, bound down outside the Gunfleet and cracking on to make sure of her turn at Ipswich; then came *Lady Daphne*, motoring, too, under topsail; Cranfield's *Anglia* newly done up and carrying full sail, with sprit squared off; *Beric*, away out in the channel; another of Cranfield's with bowsprit down and jib set; one of Goldsmith's iron pots, timber-laden; Horlock's *Adieu*, with large white topsail and a cloth or two of the mainsail picked up; Cole & Lecquire's lovely little *Henry* with a stack of timber. They were a gay, enheartening sight.

Then the skipper pointed out the bank where he once saw three magnetic mines with parachutes still attached. "They were offering five quid for a mine at the time."

"Did you get your money?"

Billy chuckled. "No, but I got a very nice letter!"

We picked up the young flood off the Blacktail Spit and stood over towards the Kent shore that showed up clear and bright in the sparkling sunshine all the way down to the North Foreland. Then we came about in the big ship channel and lay up past the Great Nore Towers into Sea Reach.

Will Everard was dropping astern, but there was another barge out ahead of us now that had just got under way. At

first she sailed stumpy fashion, with topsail clewed up, then as we overhauled her, out came her topsail sheet and the head-stick climbed slowly aloft. She was a smart barge and held us for a while.

Billy recognized her. "She'll be going on Southend with flour," he declared, and sure enough, she picked up her main-sail and stood in past the pierhead. "She's not all she seems, neither. Same as a good few others that's doubled, it's the inner skin that goes. They have to watch themselves aboard of her since she wet her cargo not so long back. That's no good loading flour and turning out dumplings!"

We made a long leg of it up Sea Reach. The breeze was freshening, and there was weight in the puffs at times. The mate had finished work below for the time being, and began an interminable walk up and down the deck, shoulders hunched up, hands in pocket, deep in thought.

Presently the skipper pointed to the weather vang. Jack nodded, and went forward to fetch a small stopped-up coil. "Jib sheets," he explained.

"That'll do."

Together they bent on the line above the upper vang fall block, and set it up on the main horse chock as a preventer. Then the skipper eased the vang fall carefully.

"That's better. I like a bit o' grass, really. That has more spring in it."

We had to make a short trip over towards the Blyth Sands to come about again just below the remains of the wartime inner boom.

"That was another awkward owd brute," Billy began, as the mainsheet block slammed and slatted across the horse. Then topsail and foresail began to fill. "All right, Jack!" The mate let fly the foresail bowline, and we were away again on the fresh tack. "Yes, we'd blown out tawps'l and fores'l coming up one day during the war, and I was having a rare owd job jilling her along under a bit o' mains'l, when jist as I was shaping up for the Gate we got put by for a collier. They didn't care. Jist laughed. That upset me, that did, so I shook my fist and shouted after them, 'Hope you sink!'

"When we got up to Beckton, blowed if she hadn't put up a mine off the jetty and killed four or five men on the fo'c'sle

150

head. That was a queer thing, that was. I'd have given anything to bring back those words."

There were barges lying in Holehaven; six of Woods' powder barges, with green rails and red outer wales, waiting for a steamer, no doubt. Coryton was busy with tankers alongside, and on the flats by the canting, disused Mucking Light, lay the shattered wreck of a tanker that had blown up during the war. "That's right, and the tug tending on her went on fire, too. The whole of the tanker's crew were lorst—all but three or four that were adrift ashore after a booze-up.

"Bombs never worried me much. If they were going to git you, they would, and that's all there was to it. I remember one night Jerry was over. Five of us lay in the Ness up along the west shore. There were searchlights either side of us. 'That's where the next one's going to come in,' I says. 'Right over the top of us.'

"He did, too. You could hear him droning away up there, then the bombs came whistling down. The first landed ahead of the other barges, and the rest blotted 'em right out. When the spray cleared, though, all five of us were still there. You'd never credit it, but the bombs had dropped between each one of us, and the larst went off jist under our starn and fairly made the owd barge jump. I tell you that shifted our water tank and never did quite go back as you can see.'

Two smart barges, *Scotsman* and *Serb,* lay at anchor in the Lower Hope with bowsprits down. In wild weather this is the last shelter before open water, and it was here that one old bargeman penned these lines to his owner:—

> "*Here we be in the Lower Hope,*
> *And when it blows we give her scope.*
> *When it eases we heave in the slack;*
> *I'm your humble servant, Timothy Black.*
>
> *P.S.—Please send us a quid.*"

Back came the reply:—

> "*What funny rhymes you bargemen make,*
> *But you'll get no quid from Mr. Drake.*"

It was coming dark as we lay up Gravesend Reach. The tide still had an hour to run, but the skipper decided it was not worth the trouble of hanging out the side lights.

There were barges already brought up off the "Ship and Lobster."

"Pick up your mains'l, Jack. . . . You might give him a hand with the lowers."

He slacked off the mainsheet, while we hove in on the brails.

"Chuck a few fathoms over the windlass barrel, Jack. Let go fores'l. . . ."

Billy unhooked the mainsheet block, then padded forward to let go the anchor. Twelve hours out from Maldon, it was the first time he had left the wheel that day.

Will Everard was just turning through the Lower Hope as he put me ashore.

"We were lucky to howd on to our tawps'l," he said, for we both knew that with *Will Everard's* bowsprit down and a bit more wind and sea it might have been a very different story. Then Billy chuckled. "Anyway, we've had a good owd sail."

CHAPTER XVI

"TALKIN' O' BARGES . . ."
A STORY OF THE OLD DAYS

TALKIN' o' barges, did you ever hear tell of Teddy Strange time he had his little ol' *Tarantella* in the barge race? Mind you, I'm going back a fair time now—fifty year or more. I was mate along o' Teddy, an' a nice ol' chap he was, too, with bushy white eyebrows an' beard. He didn't stand no more'n five foot two or three an' very quiet spoken. He never shouted nor nothing, and happen it come on to blow sudden-like: "Tom," he'd say, same as what I might be speaking to you now, "Tom, if I was you maybe I'd git that there tawps'l off of her." That's the sort of chap he was. Nothing never worried him.

Teddy was a smart sailor. He knew how to git a barge along all right. Day o' the race, there's us all dolled up in white canvas jackets and trousers and red stocking caps, and away we goes with a nice sailin' breeze so'west and everything squared off. Time we'd fetched the Mouse there's a dozen or more of us all shapin' up to gybe round in a bunch. Couple of 'em got bawsprits through their mains'ls, but ol' Teddy, he lets her run off and draw clear.

Lying tenth, we were, round the mark an' a dead beat home. Teddy fetched acrorst out o' the tide an' starts making short trips up along the Essex flats. By an' by the breeze freshens. Jest suited us, that did. That there *Tarantella* jest used to eat out to wind'ard. Time we'd turned up through Sea Reach, blowed if we ain't gorn right through the lot on 'em— all but the *Teresa* what was champion barge with a chap by the name o' Slippery Sam a-sailin' on her. Proper caution he was. Tucked us under his lee all the way up till we opened up Gravesend Reach. Reckon Sam must've figured he'd got the race in his pocket, 'cos he stands over to the Essex shore while we come about and lays over to the south'ard.

By an' by I catches sight o' Teddy with his head cocked

153

on one side an' sniffing same as somebody was a-cookin' a
nice juicy bit o' steak. Seems the breeze had southered a bit.

"We'll let her come," says Teddy quietly.

Sam, over on the other side o' the river, he sees us winding,
so he comes about in a hurry. Didn't take long to see there
was going to be precious little in it. Fust of all, it seems we're
workin' out ahead o' the *Teresa*, then she holds us. That free
puff must've bin a fluke. Nothing between the two of us, there
wasn't. 'Nother half-a-minute an' we'd be atop of each other,
an' Sam being on the starb'd tack, we'd have to give way an'
bear up under his starn, but Teddy, he kep' the *Tarantella*
rampin' full, jest as if there weren't nobody but him on the
river.

Perty soon they starts hollerin' out aboard the *Teresa*.

"I'll ram you," shouts Sam, an' I reckon he would, too,
but Teddy never so much as turned his head.

Well, I was up forrard tendin' the fores'l, but I don't mind
telling you I proper got the wind up. 'Tain't what you might
call comforting with a wicked-looking bawsprit comin' aboard
at a rate of knots. Do some damage, that can. The ol' chap we
had on the mainsheet jumped up out o' the lee scuppers an'
started bawlin' out to Teddy he'd be drowning the lot of us
if he didn't watch out. But Teddy wasn't bearin' away. Not
him! It was too late, anyway. He starts luffin' on her, holdin'
her right up into the wind.

You never saw a barge work out to weather as that there
Tarantella. She slid right along that there bawsprit end till our
fores'l give a flap, and as Teddy ups with his helm an' bore
away right acrorst *Teresa's* bows, he jest nodded towards our
mizzen an' I come runnin' aft to let fly the sheet an' top up
the boom. Jest as well I did, too! He'd only so much as to
touch us and we'd have bin out o' the race. Do you know,
that there bawsprit of his passed clean right over our rudder.

You should've heard the shout as went up aboard the steam-
boats. As fer Teddy, you might've thought he'd never heard
nothing. Even when we got our gun an' every mortal thing
on the river started soundin' off and cheering, he never took
the slightest notice, but jest beckoned fer to git the mains'l in.

That night at the supper, though. Dear, oh, dear! That was
the time, with us pilin' into blancmange an' trifle an' things

154

along of our meat an' spuds. The stuff they give us to drink! Champagne an' all. Ol' Teddy, you know he hardly touched nothin' as a rule, but you'd 'a' laughed to see him at the supper. They kep' all on fillin' up his glass. Some night, that was, I can tell you! I can't recall how we come to git back aboard. Reckon somebody must've put us off, for we'd never made it else.

Next day we didn't turn out till jest on eleven. Fust thing I done was to duck me head in a bucket o' water, but ol' Teddy, he was a sight wusser'n what I was. He come up on deck holdin' his throat an' coughin' and splutterin' somethin' awful.

"You don't look so good," I says.

"I don't feel so good, neither," he barked an' fair made me jump. His voice seemed to come right out of his boots. Proper rasp, it was.

"What about something to eat, then?" I says, jest a bit scared.

"Eat!" says he. "With me throat as dry as a bit o' salt cod! It's a drink as I'm after. Git that boat alongside an' we'll hop ashore."

"Don't you think you've had enough?" I says, for I could see by the look of him and the funny way he spoke that he hadn't got over the night before. "Shall I git you a cup o' tea?"

"Tea!" he roars. "Tea ain't no good fer a thirst like mine. Into the boat with yer!"

So ashore we goes with Teddy sittin' there croakin' an' clutchin' at his throat. He puts down a pint in the "Tartary Frigate" at one go.

"That's better," he says, then looks round an' slaps down a sovereign and calls fer drinks all round.

I could see some o' the others looking queer-like, as Teddy wasn't given to standing drinks. Couldn't make out his voice, neither. Didn't seem like him at all. Then someone comes in to say as how the gov'nor was arskin' after Teddy down at the hard.

"That's all right, mate," says Teddy. "Master knows I ain't fer away. Never no call to hurry."

By an' by I manages to git him out. Not too steady on his pins, he wasn't, but I grabs hold of his arm and helps him

along the wall. There was the gov'nor—a funny little ol' chap in a frock coat an' stove-pipe hat, with an umbrella stuck under his arm. Very strict and serious, he was, and nobody had never hardly seen him laugh. Funny gruff way of talking, he had, too.

"Good morning, Teddy," he says.

"Mornin', Master."

Now, the gov'nor had very strong views on drink, an' I could see him looking Teddy up and down.

"On the booze!" he says with a sniff.

"Well, Master, I put it to you," says Teddy, flingin' out his arms and pointin' to the *Tarantella* what's layin' off on the buoy with her champion flag flying from her spreet end. "Worth a drink, ain't she, Master?"

But the gov'nor wasn't havin' any. "You're drunk," he says.

"Me?" says Teddy, drawing hisself up as though he bin insulted. "Why, I ain't never bin drunk in me life."

"All right," says the gov'nor, "but jest you remember I'm sort o' particular about who sails them there barges o' mine."

Teddy puts his hands up and stops him.

"Master," he says very solemn and deliberate, swayin' back on his feet. "Master, if you were to tell me you wanted us to load a freight this afternoon—know what I'd say? Why, jest leave it to me, Master. That's what I'd say."

"Well," says the gov'nor, "I'm very glad to hear it. Fact is I want you to git away up an' load coal at the Albert Dock. It's urgent, that's why I come down here after you."

That was a bit of all right, that was, but Teddy never turned a hair. "Don't you worry, Master," he says, wavin' his arms like a windmill. "We'll be there. Leggo me arm, Tom. Ain't got no time to waste. Got to git a move on."

Away goes Teddy down the hard, makin' short boards till he fetches the boat. The gov'nor jest stood an' watched him fer a few moments, then tucks his gamp under his arm and stamped off.

Well, we got off to the barge all right, but what with her being light an' standin' high out o' the water, ol' Teddy couldn't git aboard. I tried heavin' him up till the pair of us very nearly landed in the water.

"Don't you worry about me," he roared. "You git sail on her. I'll stay in the boat."

156

"Oh, no, you don't," I says, an' hooked the runners in the back of his trousers. He come aboard then all right. Never turned a hair. Jest scrambled along aft and sat hisself down by the wheel.

"Up with yer anchor! " he bawled. "Haul out yer tawps'l sheet and shake out the mains'l! "

I let him git on with it. It wasn't no manner o' good payin' heed to him, so I jest took me time and got her under way. Nice little breeze no'therly, there was, and for a while Teddy sat quiet and kep' her goin'. Then a steamer comin' up astarn sounded for to pass under our lee. I could see Teddy gettin' restless. Presently, up he jumps.

"That's enough o' that row," he shouts. "Jest you pack it up," and he leaves the wheel to shake his fist at 'em.

The *Tarantella*, she starts payin' off till I thought we were going to hit the steamboat, but somehow or other we jest fetched acrorst his bows.

You should've heard what they told Teddy about hisself. Not that he took no notice, mind. Funny thing was he roared a sight more louder'n what they did—him that had never scarce lifted his voice above a whisper.

Reckon they thought he'd gorn off his head. You never heard sich a flare-up.

I was in two minds what to do. I was only a youngster at the time. Reckon I could've dropped the hook, but we were well-nigh in mid-stream. I was jest wondering what would happen if I tried taking the wheel, when blow me if ol' Billy don't take it into his head to go below..

"Where you off to? " I yelled.

"Goin' to turn in," he says, an' he did, too. Jest flaked hisself out on his bunk and was asleep in a couple o' shakes.

Proper ol' how-d'you-do, that was. I thought to meself the best thing I could do was to pull the cabin hatch to and take the barge up on me own. That wasn't so bad with a fair wind all the way up. The real awkward part was comin' alongside, but I shot her up inside the jetty an' ran forrard to let go tawps'l an' fores'l. Managed to catch a lighter a fourpenny one, but didn't do no harm.

Fust thing they wanted to know ashore was what had happened to ol' Teddy.

"He's down below," I says.

"Is he ill, then?"

"No, jest a bit under the weather. He'll be up by an' by."

He never showed up, though. They had us loaded in a couple of hours, then they wanted us away out of it. Tide was away, too, so I got a pluck down Gallions astern of a tug an' a string o' lighters. Wind was still no'therly, so I gives her the tawps'l an' fores'l an' a cloth or two o' the main, an' she jogs along down all quiet an' comfortable like.

You should've seen our decks all covered in coal. I tell you we looked some racing barge! Still had our flag up an' all, but everything come ramping down past. Not that I worried meself, for we dropped down plenty fast enough on the ebb, and time I'd brought up off the hard agen an' given the sails a rough stow, up comes ol' Teddy. I could tell by the look of him and the natural sort o' way he spoke that he was perty well hisself. He couldn't make things out at all. He looked at me an' then at the coal. Presently he says in that quiet ol' way of his:

"Where did that there coal come from, Tom?"

"Why, we've jest bin up an' loaded it."

That made him think a bit and he sat fer awhile tryin' to figure things out.

"What day was it yesterday, Tom?"

"Day o' the barge race," I says.

"So it was," and he chuckled to hisself fer a bit. Then he nods his head. "Must've bin that stuff they gave us at the supper," he murmured, then raised his voice a bit. "I didn't happen to say nothing out o' the way, like?"

"No, not to me, you didn't."

"Nor yet to Master?"

"Nothing he might take exception to. You weren't in too good shape, though."

Teddy looks hard at the coal an' sits hisself on the cabin top a-scratchin' his head. "You know, Tom," he says presently, "I reckon we might as well git ashore."

Teddy was all right now. I wasn't worried about him no more, so away we goes in the boat an' makes for the "Tartary Frigate," where Teddy calls fer a couple o' shandies. As luck would have it, who should happen to come along the wall but

the ol' gov'nor hisself. I don't reckon he'd have seen Teddy
an' me a-standin' there in the doorway but what Teddy spoke
up.

"Evenin', Master," says Teddy.

I thought the gov'nor was goin' to bust. He went the colour
o' beet, he did. Then he stumped his umbrella on the cobbles
an' fair let rip.

"You!" he shouted. "What are you doin' here?"

"Now, now," says Teddy quietly. "Don't take on so. Everything's all right."

"All right, indeed!" yelled the gov'nor, bloomin' nigh livid.
"Didn't I tell you to git away up an' load . . .?"

"Oh," says Teddy. "So that's the trouble. Why, Master,
that's the *Tarantella* a-lyin' out there now."

"I ain't blind. What about that there freight o' coal I was
on about?"

"Why, it's aboard of her, Master."

The gov'nor swung round like as if he'd been shot. He could
see fer hisself she was deep-loaded all right. He blinked an'
stared as if he was seeing things. Proper taken aback. But he
was a tough ol' boy, though. He wasn't so easily beat.

"Anyway," he says, "you're on the booze agen after what
I told you this mornin', too."

Teddy smiled that queer little smile of his an' said quietly,
"Come now, Master. I grant you I wasn't meself this mornin'
along o' that fizzy stuff they give us at the supper larst night.
Proper got me down. You ain't going to hold that against me?"

"I don't mean larst night," says the guv'nor, still a bit red
in the face.

But Teddy wasn't worrying. "There's no call to take on so,"
he says quietly, an' I see a twinkle in his eye. "Me an' Tom
here, we've only jest come ashore fer a drink same as you
might 'a' done."

I thought the gov'nor was goin' to have a fit, him a lifelong
teetotaller an' all.

"That's right, Master. Happen you'd 'a' loaded a freight
o' coal quick like, reckon you'd be glad enough to git ashore
and rinse the coal dust out o' yer throat."

The ol' gov'nor never said a word. He stamped off an' me

159

an' Teddy stood an' watched him go. Then Teddy cocks an eye aloft an' says quietly almost to hisself:

"Funny ol' weather an' no mistake. Reckon we'd better git aboard time it's quiet. Happen it'll come on to blow up nasty agen afore long."

CHAPTER XVII

AND NOW . . .

THAT the Thames sailing barge survives at all in this age of mechanization is a miracle; yet she is not to be regarded as some incongruous, out-moded anachronism, but rather as a workaday craft developed and perfected over the centuries against the commercial background of London River.

A sailorman is equally at home working above bridges with gear lowered on deck or alongside an import steamer in the docks, and from an æsthetic angle, her lofty spars and red sails give just that touch of grace and colour to complete the beauty of the scene. . . .

Tide time under the West Shore of a summer morning and the windlass pawls clank merrily as the barges shorten in; topsail headsticks climb slowly aloft to the music of patent blocks, while an old pulp-laden, red-splodged Finn glides through the placid waters, her wash slapping at the barges' leeboards and setting their rudders a-slamming. . . .

Or it may be the tang and sparkle of the Lower Hope, with a fresh north-easter blowing in from the sea, while liners, tramps and coasters pass down on the ebb and the barges heel to the weight of the breeze as they cross-tack in the jumble of a strong weather-going tide. . . .

And the Swin, too, would be a lonely, desolate waste without a barge or two cracking on for the Spitway and Ipswich River with bowsprit down and a bone in her teeth.

Most owners still have their own contract work, and in spite of competition from road and rail transport, barges still berth alongside the import steamers in the docks, thereby avoiding landing charges on transhipment cargoes of grain, flour, linseed, timber and so on for the outports.

There are slack times, of course, as in any other trade, whether it be a poor timber season or just the repercussions months later of some waterside strike on the Pacific Coast. On the whole, though, conditions are good in comparison with

those black days in the 'thirties, when barges lay for week after week on Starvation Buoys until in desperation the younger men turned elsewhere for a living. East Anglian rates are up by 120 per cent. over pre-war levels; whether, in view of the fierce road competition, they can be maintained indefinitely remains to be seen. Meanwhile, a well-found barge pays her way and the smart skipper can average £10 to £12 a week.

The difficulty has been to get the barges fitted out. At the end of the war shortage of gear was acute and barges were coming off Government service with sails blown out and worm in the bottom. Sailmakers were short-handed; many of the smaller yards had closed down and the old shipwrights retired or gone away. To get even a few barges trading again others had to be stripped of their gear and converted in their turn to motor barges, or hulked, or sold for houseboats. Many are still lying desolate and deserted on the flats.

But gradually the larger and more modern barges have been taken in hand, and in spite of the shortage of good seasoned timber, numbers have increased to some 110 barges trading under sail alone, many of them magnificent craft, such as *Verona*, rebuilt at Sittingbourne, *Anglia, Greenhithe, Cambria, Savoy, Ardeer, Reliance, Alice May, George Smeed*, and the like. The sailing barges of to-day may be getting on in years, but are as well found now as ever they were.

The modern trend is towards auxiliary power in the larger craft; this is a logical development that in no way impairs their sea-keeping qualities. *Alaric, Hydrogen, Lady Daphne, Pudge, Kathleen, Raybel* are all fine craft, and many more besides. But new diesel engines are hard to come by and expensive, too, while unreliable reconditioned engines are not worth the ship room. There are still some owners who have yet to be convinced of the desirability of power. True, the modern diesel is practically foolproof and very economical, and may serve to attract men back into barges, but the slump, when it comes —as come it must—will be the testing time. A sailorman, with insurance costing only 4/- to 5/- a day, can afford to lay on the buoys waiting for a freight, whereas the motor-barge costing 20/- to 25/- a day for insurance must of necessity be kept on the go all the time.

Sailing barges like *Mirosa* are far from finished. They are

still an economic proposition, though *Mirosa's* owners had two fine barges laid up recently, not for want of work, but for want of crews.

Writers who sentimentalize over the red sails of the Thames barges and glibly foretell their inevitable disappearance during the next year or two, by thus discouraging youngsters, are only hastening the very passing they affect to deplore. Yet there are mates' berths going for those who are willing and keen; and a smart mate can readily find a job as master.

Barge sailing is a good way of life, independent, free-and-easy, satisfying. As old John Waterhouse said: "A good barge, decent owners, and plenty of work, and I'd recommend the life to any lad." Ask Tubby Blake or George, or Captain Uglow of the *Will Everard,* who ran away from home so often that in the end his parents had to let him stay in barges. Or, better still, make a trip with such a one as Billy Austin and hear him say as I did at the end of a long day's sail: "Anyway, we had a good owd sail!"

As for ourselves, we have Peter now, a lusty two-year-old, to whom everything afloat is just a boat except for barges, and woe betide anyone who fails to recognize them! Like Elizabeth, he is very much at home sailing, and chuckles with glee when the spray starts flying. He is the right build, too, for a barge's mainsheetman.

I would like nothing better than to take the family afloat once more, and Dorothy would be willing, I think, provided we find a suitable berth. Before the war fresh water was our chief concern, and a nearby station on a London line. But there are other considerations now; we should want a permanent berth alongside, somewhere in the country, yet handy to schools and shops, with electricity and telephone as well.

It is a far cry from the day we bought *June* for £50 complete with gear and boat. Since the war there has been competition for many an old crock whose days are numbered. Even worked-out ballast barges that have been paid out in full by the clubs have sold for over £800, and barges in the dry trades are worth £1,000 and over, whatever their age.

One privately-owned old coasting barge was offered to a firm for trading at £1,000, but had to be turned down because of the dearth of crews. The owner was subsequently bid £1,300

163

for conversion to a yacht. He might have got more, so he declared afterwards, only he was so surprised that he accepted outright.

June cost about £250 to fit out as a yacht in 1933. To-day the bare cost of conversion to the most simple specification would be £1,000. New gear is two or three times pre-war prices; repairs and running costs are correspondingly high, and there is no longer the lively pre-war second-hand market in barge gear.

But the top is coming off the market for a variety of reasons. Not all who own yacht barges are sailors. Many use them merely as houseboats, and the gradual easing in the housing situation is beginning to reflect on barge prices.

I would like a bowsprit barge such as the shapely deep-sided Ipswich *Petrel,* which recently came on the market. There, indeed, would be a barge to glory in! But alas! a 120-ton barge is really too big for us to sail alone, her gear being just that much heavier to handle. On the whole, a 100-ton barge is my ideal, one that has been in the grain trade. I have in mind just such a little barge, rebuilt since the war with 24-in. hatch coamings and with hold linings and ceilings in perfect condition. No ballast drudge for me, but one that has spent her life in the clean trades, without grabs to knock her about. Mere age is no criterion. Far more important is her constitution; her builders; the sort of cargoes she carried and whether she has the reputation of a lucky barge. A hard-headed old " gripie " always in trouble is no craft for an amateur.

And having bought my barge, I would sail her to a small yard I know of where both the owner and his wife have a proper appreciation of sailing barges. I would tell what money I had to spend and decide on the essentials to be done; such things as the cabin top, bulkheads and plumbing. I would have no truck with engines, but retain the stern cabin to live in for as often and as long as we wished, and in due course I would take an old barge skipper friend aboard and rig her ourselves.

Wishful thinking, perhaps. Should the fates conspire against us and we never buy our barge, well, we have *June's* boat still, and the sea at our door. Strangely enough, I find I am more content nowadays with dreaming of sunlit days in *June*; of

oilskin weather rolling our way down Channel in coastal craft; of passages with bargemen friends up and down Swin and the London River.

Like the old-timers who frequent the sea wall alongside "The Nore," I can picture ourselves living more and more in the past as time goes by, dwelling only on the halcyon days, while all the worries and discomforts gradually fade into the limbo of the past.

We shall be as the rheumy-eyed old mariner who spent a lifetime in the old Whitstable craft at a time when life was very hard, yet can chuckle still as he yarns; like him, we, too, will harbour no regrets, but look back over the years and cheerily sigh: "They were good old times. Wet shirt—happy days! "

25th April, 1949.